It's All About Love

It's All About Love

How to Have A Better Life

Stephen Jensen

Writers Club Press

San Jose New York Lincoln Shanghai

It's All About Love
How to Have A Better Life

Writers Club Press
an imprint of iUniverse.com, Inc.

For information address:
iUniverse.com, Inc.
620 North 48th Street, Suite 201
Lincoln, NE   68504-3467
www.iuniverse.com

ISBN: 0-595-12398-8

Printed in the United States of America

*This book is dedicated to all those people who have helped me
to learn the true meaning of Love and its redeeming qualities particularly*

my teacher Lazaris—whose knowledge and love saved me from dying and

my partner Eric—whose caring and love has changed me forever

Contents

Chapter 6
—The Mental Body

Introduction

FORMAT OF THE BOOK

Everyone at some time has asked themselves one or more of the following three questions: "why is the world as it is?", "who am I?" and "can I change the world or me?" Usually they were asked before you reached the age of ten. What did you answer to these questions then and now? This book will not only answer those questions but it will tell you how you can lay the groundwork to create a truly better life for yourself so that you can have a better life.

The problem I faced in writing a book that brought together quantum science, psychology, spirituality, self help, alternative healing and metaphysics was not knowing where to start. What came first—the chicken or the egg? What was the chicken? What was the egg? Asking that question and trying to solve it is like a dog chasing its tail.

So I decided to start with what I could see out there (Division I) then move to my body because it was the constant in my life—everywhere I went it came too (Division II) then by seeing that what happened out there was directly influenced by me, I looked at how to change me so that I could change what was happening out there (Division III).

Together this gives the full picture—certainly the chicken and the egg—as everything existed either out there in the world or in me. But which is the chicken and which is the egg? Which came first? The outside world or my body or me? And if I wasn't my body then who was I? To answer the chicken and egg question the logical answer is that there must be an outside force or power greater than us or we are part of that greater or larger force. But because we are such a small part of it we cannot see that we are a part of it. Historically that greater force has been called God and the energy that God uses to create with is called LOVE. I'll call this force the Universe. No attempt at explaining life can be complete without a reference to the Universe and I too found it to be unavoidable—as hard as I tried to I had to include spirituality. All roads eventually lead there. But let's leave that until the end of Division II. The final part of this book then tells you how to heal you so that you can then create the world that you want from a place of purity, truth and Love rather than from the place of limitation that presently stops you having a better life. It will only ever be through Love that you can have what you want and be happy with it. You see life is all about Love. It is a logical and inescapable conclusion. The final Division shows you how to heal yourself on all levels—physical, emotional, mental and spiritual. This will speed up your receptivity to Love and therefore your ability to have a better life.

To expand on that then, before you can have a better life, one where you can be what you want to be and have what you want to have, you need to see the big picture. What's happening out there? There's stuff going on that you don't know about. A lot of stuff in fact. So why not see what all the options are before choosing what you want more of and what you want to change? It may be that you are wanting what you want to satisfy a part of you and don't really know why, or you may be wanting something for a reason that you are unaware of while thinking it is for another reason. This book will tell you how to answer those questions so you know you're on the right track.

You'll firstly need to know what sort of a world you are dealing with and how the world works and the impact that it has on you and you have on it. You touch on everything in your life. Division I begins by going behind what you see and looks at the intangible world of ideas, beliefs, thoughts, feelings and experiences and how these energies work together to create your reality—energy itself and the results of that energy in action and how they shape the world. If you want to be who you want to be and have what you want to have then you need to know how the world works. You need to know what you are dealing with.

Then you need to know who it is that is this "you" that lives in this world (Division II will tell you that). Together you can then be in an informed position to choose how to have a better life because now you will have the big picture. Division III is all about house keeping so you can be clear to receive the Love.

In the process of getting to the answer to the question "who am I" this will raise more questions, like "how far back in my past do I go to find out?" And "what is the relevant event or cause of what I am now?" And "where did I start?" Then it gets just plain complicated, and most people get lost or give up and go back to their daily lives looking for other solutions to their problems and questions. This book will deftly take you through that maze of questions so you don't get lost or confused and the solution becomes abundantly clear.

The solution to this maze is to use a metaphysical framework—a map or guide book as a reference. Metaphysics works within a holistic point of view, i.e. it combines everything that is both hidden or non-physical with the physical world that we all experience with our five senses. I know from my own experience that metaphysics works and that it is a real explanation for how reality works. It is the how, when and wherefore behind what we sense and experience. You're going to enjoy working with it. It makes so much sense and when you do get the answers there will be a realization within you that you always had the answers but that you had forgotten them. Then you'll know you're on the right path.

Metaphysics looks at the energy fields that make up the human and impact on it. More relevant than most people know is the energy of Martyr and Victimhood—both are tools of self punishment that stop us receiving the Love we need to have before our lives can improve. Most people aren't aware that they are even doing it. Anyone who has blamed has played Victim. The basis of self knowledge is taking responsibility for your own lives. Therefore, in order to do that, Victimhood can no longer be part of your life. There isn't a person alive today who has not had to deal with Guilt and Self Pity and these are also examined. These emotional blockages of your energy create disease. More importantly they are strong causes of stopping you from being more of the real you and from getting in touch with the Love you need—the fuel—to make the changes that you need to in order to have a better life.

Most people on the planet today are letting limited aspects of who they think they are to control and direct them. They think they know what they want but because they really don't know who they are, they can't know what the whole or real them wants. They are being directed by a limited aspect of themselves. It is said that they are "asleep" and this applies to most people on the Planet. That type of life is based on one energy—FEAR. Often behaviors are put in place to stop you feeling this Fear (and anything else for that matter) and so you are even more unaware of your lack of self awareness. It can be self induced through obsessive compulsive disorders or through addiction. Anything in fact that stops you feeling or experiencing. An addiction is anything that stops you growing internally as a person through behavior that numbs your feelings e.g. "can't live without my caffeine, alcohol, nicotine or sugar hits each day" just to mention a few. In order to know who you are you will need to go beyond Fear. Again, this is not a painful experience.

By finding out who you are you will learn who you want to be. The process will tell you why you do what you do. Then you will be free to choose to do or not to do what you have been doing. This book will give you this information and the tools needed for self discovery and self and life creation. It is in the outside world that you will find your first clues for finding out who you are at this moment in time and that is why I have started the book there. Knowing who you are lets you be free to take the next step of finding out who your real self is—the part of you that has the Love and isn't afraid.

In learning who you are, you will touch the essence of who you were in the beginning and who you really are and always were—at the moment you are not in touch with that part of yourself—this is the source of Love. In the beginning you were the innocent being who started out in life with dreams and fantasies but who had to change over the years and who had to become something else. And you lost that original person under the influences of what I call "the usual suspects"—parents, school, church, work, society, government and your peers. You ended up not quite sure of why you were doing what you were doing. Who would you have been if certain things hadn't happened to you and can you change back into that person? And you will learn why those things happened to change you. Those answers are in you and this book will show you how to find them. This is not a painful experience.

Now you will be free to change what you do and have what this new you wants to have. The only things you will cease to have are those that hurt you and create unhappiness in your life. So it's a pretty good deal. Division III shows you how to change you. Here are the techniques on how to clear the blockages and identify parts of yourself that you have not previously been aware of. This is the hands on section of the book. The more stuff you clear away the more Love you let in. It's like making a hole in a dam. Eventually the amount of water gushing out of the dam demolishes the rest of the wall. Love is the same. As you clear away more Love comes through and burns away the blockages. It's a rapid process once it starts. Before you know it you're feeling better than you ever have before and life is wonderful like you've never known. You now have a better life and it was all about Love.

BE INSPIRED

As a result of the outside influences of the world, some people have already given up on living their lives. We see them energyless, shuffling through life, ill, lapsed into decaying habits, burdened and worried, angry, grown resentful of others, bitter, pessimistic and struggling to the point of hopelessness through their powerlessness. Others have settled for mediocrity and its safeness—"don't rock the boat" attitudes. Just surviving from pay day to pay day—always having one eye on tomorrow and the other over their shoulder on the past. But never really being happy with what is happening now. And if they are—it's only for a little while at a time.

But there are those who have moved beyond the Fear of limitation, who live richly rewarding lives. Although it would be denied by most, that is the life that we all want. It is in fact the one available to everyone but it has been chosen and accepted by only those who were willing to have it. This book will make you aware of this willingness and how to have the life that the real you really wants.

From a knowledge of what this book provides, the application of that knowledge, and its use, you can accelerate your growth as a person, develop the life that you really want and heal your diseases and ill-ateases. Some of you are sick. Illness is also part of finding out who you are—a more in your face situation to deal with and that in itself can be beneficial—your body is giving you clues as to what issues you should be looking at. In many ways you have a head start in finding out who you are. So knowing who you are is the next step to being able to know how to fix yourself—because in learning how you are put together you will have learnt what is out of balance with you. Knowing who you are will reveal the answers to such questions as the cause of disease and how to heal yourself. Division III brings the information from Divisions I & II and applies that so as to show you how to heal yourself and in so doing letting you become your true self. This is a strong claim but validated time and again throughout the book.

This book is also all about waking you up to who you really are and of you optimizing your potential to being a successful person—whatever that may be for you. To being fully self aware. To being conscious. Once conscious you can start accessing parts of your consciousness which are dormant or unknown to you at the moment. Aspects that make you more of your real self and not just the Ego based identity that is seen to be Bill Jones or Jenny Smith. This is when you will really start to evolve as a human being and resume the position as creator that it was always intended that you would occupy—and not be some zombie at the effect of all around him, diseased, dazed and dormant. Fearful as that may sound it is actually an exciting prospect. This is one reason why now you cannot imagine what your life will be like and how it will change when you become self aware. You will go from being a passenger on the bus of mass consciousness to being the driver of your very own custom designed, hand made car. It is time to get off the bus and take the controls of your destiny. Master of your own domain.

This book will be whatever you want it to be—confronting and/or an affront to some, Anger producing to others, a curiosity—especially those who are waiting to be rescued. To others it will be what they have been looking for—whether they know it or not—or a trigger to explore themselves further. Whatever meaning you put on it, it is offered sincerely as an aid to help you come to terms more fully with yourself. Metaphysics is working for me, and from my experience in helping those around me, it is working for them too.

What is put to you in this book is based on my beliefs and you are free to accept or reject all or any part of what I say. I have no formal or informal training in medicine or healing. I do not belong to nor am I am affiliated with any Church or religious group or spiritual organization so I have no one else's drum to beat. It is my belief that I do not need to be part of a larger body to support me. My emotional and spiritual support comes from Love—Self Love and from the Love of others.

Today I live with a richness of experience that allows me to value life as a precious gift free of the struggle that I previously endured and thought essential to being liked but which really did not serve me. I am a totally different person. My life is fabulous. In the re-evaluation of life I now have compassion. My whole life has changed in ways that I could not have imagined when I was the old me. There is a level of self-esteem, Self Love, self acceptance, self-worth, freedom from shame and Guilt and an openness and acceptance of who I am, that is not only nurturing but empowering, and generating a Lightness of Being that cannot be described but only felt. A lightness that comes from the light of knowledge and being out of the shadow of Fear, Anger and ignorance. I feel like a huge burden that I had been carrying for years, one that got heavier as I got older, has been lifted from me.

Finding out who you are is a truly transforming experience. After you do you will never see life nor yourself the same way again. It is impossible to do so. I can guarantee it.

My path took me from marketing into advertising to psychology, human behavior and sociology, then into metaphysics and the power and function of thought and feeling, then into the being and doing energy that is the basis of our reality and from them to the concepts of God and Goddess and in turn back to the very Source of all unified energy—All That Is, the Universe, Wholeness, Oneness. I learned that what I was seeing in metaphysics was filtering down into society as sociology and psychology and in turn further down into marketing principles and that people were being taught at this level. Art was merely an expression of feeling and a reflection of life. This in turn through the dramatic arts, television and cinema were teaching people who they were by putting up a mirror for them to see. Self awareness courses began to incorporate the lessons of metaphysics. Eventually it became abundantly clear that all personal development courses were based on the principles of metaphysics and in turn spirituality itself.

The opportunity to find out who you are starts now by picking up this book and being open minded enough to finish reading it. You have nothing to loose. Sometimes when we feel well, we forget that it is our life that is at stake. It is easier to prevent dis-ease than it is to heal it—and cheaper and less painful too. If you are into self punishment though it isn't always easy to pass by the allure of illness. Metaphysics will make you aware of that pattern.

Welcome.

DIVISION I

—THE WORLD OUTSIDE YOU

Chapter 1

—POLARITY

We all see the world from a perspective of "me" and "the world out there." That is to say "I am in the world". Whenever we are "I" this immediately separates us from the rest of everything that is not "I". The whole world therefore is a world of "I" and "not I". This "I" is personified and called "Ego". The Ego therefore separates us from the world around us. It does this by analyzing, judging and choosing. I talk a lot about Ego in this book. An understanding of it is crucial to having a better life and healing yourself. Let me mention now that when I talk I talk of Ego I am referring to the negative aspect of it—what can only be called "bad". It is the ugly face we see in mankind. In the section on Ego you will see that it is the part of you that is detrimental to you and which wants to hurt you—whether you know it or not. Later in the chapter on Ego all facets of this negativity is explored. I am not talking about the positive aspect of Ego—that which gives you your individuality. The part of you that makes you different from everyone else on Earth.

In life we can put the word "not" before everything. Our consciousness has been trained to split everything into opposites, forcing us to decide between that which is and that which is not, e.g. yes/not yes (or no), black/not black (or white) and right/not right (or wrong). These choices we can experience as conflict, i.e. which one "should" we choose. Therefore this "I" also lives in a world of opposites, i.e.—a world that is divided—a polarized world.

So we not only dissect the world from a point of view of "me" and "you" but we then further divide "you" more and more based on what is right or on what we should be doing to name just two basis for making a judgment. The end result is the creation of a world of separateness or what is called "separation" from what was previously called the "whole". Splitting the atom is a good analogy. The result is that the more we separate, we become more insulated and more distinctive, e.g. in our society, Ego drives the development of the person and as we mature into adulthood the eccentricities become more obvious. On the other hand, in a closed society where the identity forgoes or limits this Egoic development the more homogenous the person becomes, e.g. in a religious order—even though the order is in itself very separate and sometimes isolated from society (because of its choices for expression of its choices). Limits on free will and creativity will have the same effect.

You would have noticed the underlying theme of almost all classic literature and film—the struggle between two opposing poles. Art reflects life back to us. If you can't see what is going on in life look in TV drama. These plays are presented in the form of two-dimensional illusions. They started as black and white (which is as polarized and as in your face as you can get) so that we could see the picture clearly and abstractly—with no distraction from the color of our world—the color of emotion. As we became more emotionally aware we began to see our dramas in colored television. TV is used as the medium that shows us the intimate real life aspects of our daily lives. The movies are the medium that shows us an imagination and a world that is "larger than life"—epitomized by the size of the movie screen.

The most basic struggle in religion and literature is between good and evil, light and dark, right and wrong. The merits of this struggle are subjective, i.e. it is based on our own opinion or moral judgment and this dissection forms the ultimate basis of all decisions on Earth. It is a divisive and destructive means of creation that leads to death. Splitting the atom unleashed the power that the whole atom had contained. If atoms were merged (fusion as opposed to fission) and not split then surely this would yield even greater power; and that does not take into account the synergistic effect. Fusion is a probability for Earth and would answer all our power needs. The power from Hydrogen (a building block of the Universe) alone is sufficient to yield all our power needs. But for reasons, which are explained later, we need to make our consciousness whole and unpolarized, so that fusion will be a reflection of the new emerging reality that we want to create. In many ways it is as obvious as the nose on your face. This is perhaps why we have not seen it or because we were told that we can't see it. If you look at the merging of the male and female energy you also have creation—a child. Divorce traditionally always has been associated with heartache so why would we create our world from heartache when we could create it from Love?

Another by-product of choosing separateness is that the more separate we become the more Fear we encounter. The more Fear that is encountered the more insecure a person becomes and the more they resist change. They are afraid to move. You will notice how much older people resist change. One of the only constants in life is change, so the more you try and resist change the harder it is to do so and the more frightened you become in your motivation and basis for making choices. The more you resist change, the more that change occurs around you, thus heightening the Fear. It is a sense of loosing control and not understanding what is going on around you. It becomes a vicious cycle that leads to stagnation and paralysis and finally to death when all of you stops moving—swallowed by Fear. You are therefore killing yourself in avoiding wholeness.

The truth is that no choice is ever right or wrong—in its purest sense it is only a choice. Our Ego-based judgments have merely valued them as being right or wrong. But who is to say what is right and what is wrong? God on Judgment Day? I do not believe that. I believe that we judge and that without judging everything is without labels and part of a whole.

We live in a polarized world—a world of opposites—always moving from one to the other in one way or another. To have a better life means that something in your present life has to change—to be healed. Any reference to healing therefore is a reference to changing something in your life that you think is wrong and you want to be different. I talk about healing and disease a lot in this book and this is what I mean by it. Healing is thus a process that takes us out of polarity and into unity or wholeness. In other words "leaving the world behind", so as to "transcend" the polarity. To do this we have to let go of the "I" or the Ego which divides us from the rest of existence. Seeking a healing within the polarity is destined to certain failure. You can't heal in a polarized system. Whenever you choose one pole you are denying the other. This denial energy then gets a life of its own and that in turn becomes another problem to solve in the healing. I talk about this in The Shadow in Chapter 6.3. You have to choose both polarities simultaneously. In a polarized world you always have to choose—even no choice is a choice not to choose and is therefore a choice in itself. So choice is always being made.

We all believe that we are good and right and we want to spend our time convincing other people that they should share our belief system because then all the World would be good and right. Look at the polarity of politics. Left wing and right wing and how government passes from one to the other. After years of left wing politicians we then choose a right wing government. Traditionally one spends and the other saves. One fosters materialistic progress while the other is more open to the arts. Form as opposed to essence. It is always opposites— although these days they both seem to be the same. More proof that we are moving beyond polarity?

The more we try to prove right and wrong, good and evil, God and the devil etc. the more deeply we dig ourselves into polarity and the further we take ourselves into imbalance or what could be called illness and away from overcoming illness. And this illness doesn't mean just our health—it means the environment too, social disorder and moral decay. Everything that you would call "bad". So the concept of healing that I have referred to above becomes relevant again.

Eventually war breaks out between the two poles when we are too entrenched in one polarity especially where we are trying hard to convince others and the others are holding an extremely opposite view to us. There's a build up of friction or energy. There can be no peace until there is no polarity. It is the magnetism within the polarized field that keeps the energy moving. Once polarity is removed then there is no conflict to produce war—and I just don't mean physical war—bur war within the environment or society. And this applies to our internal war also—the one from which disease arises. Internal conflicts are always played out as external conflicts anyway—so war is a result of our own disease. The belief in polarity is carried in the Unconscious Mind of almost every one on the Planet. Ultimately polarity is only thoughts and it is here that polarity needs to be dealt with—not "out there" in the world that you see. You see everything is in the Mind and the Mind is much more than you previously imagined it to be. It goes beyond the brain, memory and abstract thoughts. It is based in your Causal Body—an energy field that circles you and which is explained in Chapter 7.

On the whole, people can't see this and because they feel alive when they are impassioned about their point of view, and therefore convinced that it is right, the more strongly they feel about them and the more they pursue their polarized views. The stronger the view is held, the greater the risk of conflict with someone who holds an opposite view.

The only way around this endless, timeless merry-go-round of polarity, good and bad and right and wrong is to rise above it. Unity will combine all the opposites and so by excluding nothing, we can become whole and therefore healed.

The place of no polarity is wholeness—the only place where disease can't exist. The use of the term holistic or holistic medicine has its basis in this philosophy. This book is concerned in helping to take you back to a place of wholeness so that there is no disease or illness—a place where you can create a better life.

One of the only things in the Universe that can be changed is the way in which we see. We have been stuck in a system that says that the only way to change anything is to change it on the outside by doing something about it—in metaphysics this is called using male energy (the energy of doing)—that is why men have ruled this Planet. It was a society based on strength—survival of the fittest. It isn't working too well at the moment—war, environmental destruction, famine, disease and Fear are rife. To bring this situation into balance would require a balancing of the female energy with the male energy so as to form Wholeness. Fortunately that is happening. In the last 100 years women have begun to take back their rights and are being recognized as leaders. But that is just swapping one polarity for another. However the female brings Love and it is this difference which will heal the polarity—Love transcends polarity. So if you want to have a better life it is all about Love.

There is a saying—the more things change, the more things stay the same. Patterns repeat themselves. History repeats itself. Over and over again. This is called the Law of Complementarity. This preserves the balance of the poles. Breathing out always follows breathing in. The way that things happen change from time to time—different wars have used different strategies and arms but in the end they are just wars. People still pollute their own environment and clean it up again but pollution is pollution whatever form it takes. In other words the more things change the more they stay the same.

This then is the world of our Planet—our physical world—the world that we look out to—the Outer World of the Third Dimension. There is also the world that is the opposite of this—the non-physical or hidden or Inner World—the world that exists within us that we look into. This is the world that needs to be made whole again and I will explain why in the next Chapter. So much focus in Western Medicine has been on the Outer World while medicine in the East has focused on the Inner World. Holistic medicine or what is now called integrated medicine seeks to combine the two of them. Wholeness is now the name of the game. Becoming One is the future. This direction is now being played out in the world through the concept of the Global Village, global awareness, the Internet, planetary survival, the breakdown of national boundaries and cultures. It is happening in spite of Fear and the wanting of people to hold onto the past and the conflict that that produces in the world. The separateness of every-thing is merging.

For a more full explanation of polarity you should read *The Healing Power of Illness* (1995) by Thorwald Dethlefsen & Rüdiger Dahlke published by Element Book. It is really a very good book with lots of detailed information about many diseases and their emotional causes.

Chapter 2

—CREATING YOUR OWN REALITY

2.1   WHAT IS REALITY NOW?

Reality is what you think it is. Reality is what you perceive and think is real. You can share it with others in what is called the consensus reality, i.e. a reality where we all agree on what is happening. Or it can be a world in which only you live in. In either event, reality is your life.

Reality has four components—

1.   **Frozen thoughts**—your world is what you think it is. Your thoughts are translated into physical objects that you can touch, eat, see, hear and smell.

2.   **Feelings** (which includes emotions)

3.   **Beliefs**

4.   **Mysticism**—the glue that ties all four together.

Until 1400–1500 AD all 4 were held to be *real*. All were in a circle and woven together. There was no discrimination between each of them. This created a synergy. Then the Renaissance happened. Science and religion (which was politically expanding at the time) joined together to take over the world.

Science eliminated thoughts and kept things, and things became real.

Religion took belief and attitudes and called it faith. Beliefs and attitudes can be changed, amended, altered. This was dangerous to an organization that needed your complete attention. But you can't challenge faith. You are a sinner if you do. You don't question faith. The Church would kill you if you didn't believe what they said, e.g. the big ones being the Spanish Inquisition, the religious wars of the Reformation, the Crusades, and the non-descript ones being all those subtle societal and peer pressures from within the Church that ebb and flow around you. Religion claimed it was real too. So both science and religion proclaimed themselves to be the one true God and sought your hearts and minds. Both claimed that the other wasn't real.

Emotion isn't predictable so science didn't like it. It wasn't quantifiable. It wasn't recordable. Religion didn't like mysticism and believed that anything that was not understandable had to be of the devil. If it goes against faith its of the devil. So religion and science agreed that feelings, and mysticism, had to go but they couldn't get rid of them all together. Metaphysics is defined at that which is beyond the real world and it was outcast as being mysticism. In historical terms the study of both mysticism and feelings are increasing. The English tradition of stiff upper lip has given way to Freud and Jung and day time soap operas which are all about understanding emotions and personal conflict.

You can't understand a set of which you are a member. You have to stand outside of it. Science is a set within thoughts, feelings, beliefs and mysticism and so is Religion. So feelings and mysticism can't understand Science and Religion. It is within the set of the four reality components. Convention says that science is real and that religion is all the rest. Try and remember that it was only the 1970's that the Catholic Church took Gallileo off its criminal list—such has been the chasm, distrust and dislike between science and religion.

But fundamental shifts began to occur in Vatican II (pity it closed before the subject of sex was reached and the Church remained in the Middle Ages), then in the Social revolution of the 60's, the 70's, the 80's and 90's as we moved further into the New Age and the astrological Age of Acquarius. Science, through quantum physics, quantum chemistry and quantum biology is trying to prove the unreality of religion. As early as 1929-30 it was suggested that reality is a product of thoughts.

Religion on the other hand is becoming fundamentalist.

As the world becomes more unreal—faith becomes more real—then science and religion will swap places. Feelings and mysticism will return as valuable concepts and mysticism will become an explanation for the workings of the world and all 4 aspects of reality will become *unreal*. A complete about face will have happened. This book is an attempt to explain science, religion and feelings from a mystical and metaphysical basis. In this New Renaissance that we are now in the divisive work of the Renaissance will be undone. As science searches for its "Unified Theory" and finds less and less theories to explain more and more science, metaphysics will provide the answer one day.

This is where the New Age is going and this about face is happening now. Many people are becoming aware of the alienation—feeling separate from the rest—feeling the world closing in on them. Love is now a necessity for survival. It is a survival tool. The world is in upheaval turning upside down being stretched and pulled apart. If you do not know what is happening around you, it is a potential nightmare with the potential to produce more Fear. It is a playground if you do know what is happening. Metaphysics creates order out of disorder. It is the glue that holds reality together. Once you understand metaphysics then you will understand what is happening around you and why. And I guarantee you that life will become incredibly simpler. The old way of linear thinking no longer works into today's emerging multidimensional world.

The old order of right and wrong, family values and stability are changing in this rearrangement of reality. The conservatives who hate change are afraid and the more they try to hold on in the midst of this change the more frightened they become. This Fear based reality holds the keys to conflicts that could be used by this group to hold onto their past. But it is inevitable that fundamental change is here to stay. Reality is becoming a multi-dimensional soup. Look at how web sites are created and presented to you—it is a multi dimensional illusion that rises and falls in and on itself, under and through itself, a highway on which you can be in more than one place at a time—that is being multi-dimensional. How many web sites can you have open at the one time? The outside world is becoming the same way, e.g. the lines of gender are shifting and often we don't know where one thing starts and another finishes. Today's trendy heterosexual man would have been seen as being gay 20 years ago, had he presented then as he does today. More than that, he would probably have been arrested for his appearance and behavior.

As a society we have been systematically removing the boundaries that separate us from one another—race, religion, gender, sexual orientation, disability. America has become the melting pot of the world so far as this is concerned. Art has reflected this in removing the boundaries between form and merging all information into one "eye-full". I'm waiting for the movie that plays two or more movies simultaneously on the same screen. TV does it already. Our capacity to understand and assimilate is increasing.

This New World, that is emerging, is a reflection of an expanding consciousness, where you are learning to access parts of your brain never before accessed. You no longer think in a linear two-dimensional fashion. You have started thinking 5th dimensionally—where everything happens simultaneously. Look at how graphics are now presented on a page—it's everything at once; another example of art reflecting the reality of boundary less form. We are removing rigidity from society. Social control mechanisms are being disbanded, e.g. the institution of marriage, dress conformity, moral behavior, birth control, genetic engineering. You can't have order in that world. It is chaos. Which is what the Universe is. And within the chaos there is order. Peak hour pedestrian traffic in the big city looks terribly chaotic but there is order within it. Same with a football game. You see people running everywhere but everyone on the field knows where they are going. Each knows his purpose. And the old skill of B follows A will work less and less in the world. The rigid rules and patterns are not there any more. You need new skills in order to survive, so as not be overwhelmed by the stress from the uncertainty of an uncertain future. Predictability is yesterday's luxury. Love is tomorrow's answer. It was always the answer but now it is imperative for survival. If we are going to play God and create this New World then we will need to have plenty of compassion and Love or it will be doomed to pain and struggle, limitation and lack. The stress will kill you. In fact it has already started killing people.

Because you live in the set you don't see how over the last 20 years the definition of reality has been pulled apart. In the last 20 years 90% of all knowledge was discovered. Take a moment to digest that statistic. The only quality that applied to all 4 (frozen thoughts, feelings, beliefs, and mysticism) is **Love** to keep it all together and to make it make sense. Many people deal with this oncoming New Age by being numb. I talk about the impact of that in Chapter 5.6. They feel nothing and don't think or have attitudes or beliefs for themselves. They are energy sucking robots stuck in Negative Ego in a Fear based reality at effect in their lives. Ever wondered why you get so tired being around certain people? It is no longer possible to survive in the world with that mentality. It is fatal. We are living in a fastly evolving New World that requires each of us to be in harmony and balance with all around us. A harmony and balance that we create. Disharmony causes disease. A polarized world such as earth is mostly in disharmony.

2.2   BELIEF CREATES REALITY

Can I tell you of a few things that I believe about the Mind?
1. **Your Mind doesn't think by itself**—you think using your Mind—it's a tool and it's up to you as to how you use it.
2. **Your Mind has been analyzed into components**—a number of which include Ego, Conscious Mind, Shadow, Subconscious Mind, Unconscious Mind, Child, Adolescent and Young Adult. You are using each of these and other aspects of your Mind to think all the time. You have given each aspect its own agenda.

However, any differentiation or meaning given to that aspect of Mind isn't really relevant when trying to understand the thought. This is the opposite of what a psychoanalyst would tell you. As analysts it is their job to analyze, to divide, to dissect and then to re-assemble in a way that explains thoughts. That was helpful in getting us to this place of understanding of Mind but I now believe we have moved past this rudimentary form of analysis and are educated enough to recognize that a thought is a thought is a thought—whatever part of the Mind that it comes from. This means that it doesn't matter if it was from this or that aspect of the Mind that the thought came. Thoughts come and thoughts go. But it's the thoughts that you believe that matter most because it is at this point that you are choosing a polarity and at the same time not choosing its opposite. This is the important fact about thoughts—not where they came from. And once the thought is identified then that is just the start of the reality creation process as I propose it exists.

3. **You have empowered your thoughts with beliefs**. In other words, you don't believe every thought that you have. Some of your beliefs are stronger than others, e.g. "I want a new car" but you have a conflicting belief that says, "I don't deserve a new car because I am not good enough or haven't worked hard enough to deserve it". Or, you don't have the money. Or, you have given more power to a belief from which you receive a hidden benefit called a pay off. This is a benefit that you aren't consciously aware of and I'll talk more about them in Chapter 5. For instance, you have a belief that you are not good enough and this justifies you having Self Pity. This then fuels other people feeling sorry for you. This then is how you manipulate your reality to get what you want. In this case it is to have attention/Love. The pay off of receiving the attention/Love is too good for you to want to give up the Self Pity or the belief in yourself that you are not good enough. By putting together the examples of the beliefs, you'll see that you can't get the new car because you are getting Love

instead by using Self Pity and if you had a car then you couldn't have the Love. What will become clear later is that by creating a new belief and dropping the Self Pity, then you can have both the new car and Love. In other words, you can have it all and know why. The point is that for various reasons you have empowered your thoughts by making them into beliefs.

By thinking something, we project that thought energy out into our Outer World, and therefore have impact on the world (or what I'll call the "energy field") that we are in. As you know, different energy vibrates at different resonances. Earth is a planet of dual polarity as we have seen (a dimension of opposites—on/off, yes/no, north/south— and the formula for anything trendy is the cutting and pasting together of inconsistent polarities—also called Post Modernism).

The law of attraction is that similar energy attracts similar energy, i.e. those resonating most like each other will attract each other. Birds of a feather flock together. Winners mix with winners etc. Look at any gathering of people at any event where there is a common purpose— the ABC bar crowd as opposed to the XYZ bar crowd and you'll see that the people who frequent particular places all have something in common, e.g. a convention of people—travel agents, bank managers, lawyers etc. (they may even all look like one another because of their clothing style, make up, age). All may be diverse within the grouping (and therefore it looks like chaos) but all are mentally connected by the deeper traits of common purpose, attitude and belief. This law of attraction goes beyond socio-economic identification and includes emotional states as well as belief states. So if I believe that I am power- less then I will attract to me either/or another powerless person, or event or thing that reinforces my powerlessness. And this could appear before you as something to which you are addicted. Addiction keeps you powerless. So the experience of the de-powering event will be the experience that you have because of your belief. It doesn't mat- ter where your beliefs come from. Just as thoughts are only thoughts. Beliefs are only beliefs. They should not be judged as being good or bad but merely recognized for what they are. Your emotional state is caused by your beliefs too. As to why, I will explain shortly.

As for the law that opposites attract, this is based on the denied aspects of you that you are manifesting in front of you. This concept will be explored fully in Chapter 6.3 The Shadow. It isn't really the opposite of you but that part of you that you don't admit. It is polarity at work. As I have said earlier—the more you choose one thing the more you create it's opposite in the Shadow. Nature works to complete itself. One polarity always seeks its opposite. The effect of this is to bring the polarity into balance.

Mathematically this could be expressed as one plus minus one equals zero. $1 + -1 = 0$.

2.3   CHECKING BELIEFS

So the first thing that you need to do is to find out what your beliefs are. As mentioned above, you may find that you have conflicting beliefs. Often behind a belief there is a supporting belief and under that there is another. Eventually you will come down to your core beliefs. The ones that under pin everything. Quite often all your beliefs can be summarized down into a handful of beliefs. Everything else is just an example of how complicated you've let your life become.

Sometimes as a coping mechanism with life you simply denied everything and formed a belief that to deal with life it would be safer just to stay rigid, to have fixed views that you wouldn't be challenged on. And you stick by that even if it means cutting off your nose to spite your face. Or you run a mile when challenged rather than have to expand your Mind or face the possibility that there is another way. This way you are safe in your world of beliefs and will righteously argue that until the day you die. The bottom line is that these are just belief systems. They vary from culture to culture and even from city to city in the same culture. One day capital punishment is in vogue, yet years later it is not. Who is to say what are wrong beliefs and what are right beliefs? Bottom line is that they are only beliefs.

Have you ever asked the question—"who am I?" Are you the sum of your beliefs? Do you want to know who you are? Do you have the courage to ask? I can tell you now—you have nothing to fear. When you do find out who you are then you will wonder why you had hesitated to ask before. Because what you find will give you so much joy and peace. It is your beliefs that tell you otherwise and your Fear that causes you to doubt.

It is now time to discover who you are so as to acquire self knowledge and then once empowered by that being able to create the life that you truly want to have.

There is a lot going on in your head. In today's world that can almost be inevitable but it doesn't have to be so. As we get older we find more to complicate our lives—either with personal drama, illness, or by just thinking about or getting involved with being in the world and the negative view of it that we are continually given by the mass media. Many people do this because they can't bear to be still. It is too frightening to sit and think. They act scared and have to keep moving. People generally try and avoid the looking inwards of self-awareness afraid of what they might find. Ironically Fear is only a fog that hides the treasure that sits behind it—Love. They look outward into the world for their answers. Out there they will only ever find clues to the answers. The answers lie within.

So the world gets faster and more complicated and the boundaries come down and everything gets confusing and overwhelming for a lot of people. But this is one explanation for a faster world. Evolving consciousness is the other. As more people become self-aware they find new ways of living in the world and being at peace within themselves. They have learned what this book attempts to explain—that in this new way of coping with the world they are able to create more quickly what they want and that what they believe manifests more quickly in front of them—almost by magic. It is this quickening that we all now experience but which the unself-aware do not understand and therefore are frightened of.

If your consciousness is not also evolving then you will become more afraid and do more to assuage that Fear. The end result of that is inevitable—you will become diseased and not have as good a life as you want. You'll see too many people having a better time than you. So the choice is now yours. You are at a crossroads. Do you look within, become self aware, and thereby raise your consciousness so that you can deal with your world and let it become a New World? Or do you continue to look out into the world, trying to make sense of it but not knowing for sure that what you are doing is right? Even if you are sure of it can you really know? Everything after all is subjective. That in itself should be a clue to you to stop and at least look at where your thinking or rationalization begins. And if you can't say that you are perfectly at peace and have everything that you want—then how do you get to have a better life? You need to look at what you have created in your life before you can answer this question.

For those of you who are not completely self aware all the time then some internal work has to be done so that you can get in touch with who you are so that you can learn what your beliefs are and thereby be truly free to create your own reality. What you now need to realize is that all along you have been creating your own reality. You have had choices. You have made decisions even when you thought you weren't. Non choice is a decision not to choose and is therefore a choice too. Sometimes you may not have been aware of all the choices, e.g. you did not consider that death, losing the job, staying with your spouse or whatever as being options—but they were. You just wouldn't let yourself have them. But when free of the influences of the various aspects of yourself you will be free to actually consciously create your own world. One that is balanced and free of disease.

Healing your emotions will assist you in finding out your beliefs. I believe that one needs to understand the background to what is happening, to see the bigger picture and have a context in which to understand. Metaphysics is a philosophical context in which to make sense of the world so that you can see your beliefs. It is your beliefs that empower your thoughts. Thoughts mean nothing without empowerment from beliefs. It is vital to understand this.

To find out what your beliefs are you need to see what your experiences are. One is connected to the other, e.g. if you believe "that rainy days are nasty days and that if it is a rainy day then you won't be happy when you wake up and see that" what do you expect your experience will be when you wake up? On the other hand if you don't believe that rainy days will put you in a bad mood then clearly you shouldn't wake up unhappy. So the test of a belief is to look at your experience and to ask yourself "what must my belief have been for me to have experienced that?" I would not expect that you could at this point answer the question. It's not that easy an exercise unless you can see the full picture. And the full picture includes being able to recognize your Shadow and your Ego at work and being able to identify your emotions. Later chapters will show you very clearly how to do this.

2.4   BELIEFS PRECEDE EXPERIENCE

So we have a situation now where we can see that experience and beliefs are related. First we have the thought, which we believe or not, e.g. "I am not going to get the job that I am applying for". Then we have the experience of the belief. It is not the other way around. The experience reinforces the belief. Makes it stronger. While we may learn lessons from our experiences and new beliefs form from them—our experiences are the result of our beliefs. This is a big break through in understanding how you create your own reality.

The experience proves the belief to be true. So if something happens to you, e.g. you contract a disease. You have to ask yourself—what must have been my belief in order for me to be out of balance and therefore open to contracting that particular disease?

Beliefs can't be changed but new beliefs can be formed. It's all a matter of how strongly you believe. It's your will and desire—your intention—that matters. Once the belief is in place—it is stored in your body on a cellular level and in turn in your DNA—then like computer hard drives, the information can be written over but it always stays in memory. So the old beliefs will always be in your memory. And if the old beliefs become strong enough and other factors are in place then your body will reproduce the conditions in your life that were there when the beliefs were formed.

So if you want to change your experience, then create new beliefs. New beliefs will attract a new reality to you. Remember that similar resonance attracts similar resonance. This is my experience. It can be yours too. It really works and it really is that simple. If you believe that it will be hard or has to be hard then it will be so. But it doesn't have to be. It is your belief in struggle, hard work, that things take time and miracles being only for the desperate that won't allow you to have what you want.

And while on that subject think about this—when you ask yourself "who am I" do you also wonder why you are as you are? What made you? Who is this person that is asking the question "who am I?" If you didn't have the beliefs that you did would you be someone else? And then do you not wonder: "which part of me is wanting these beliefs to be changed?" And is it a part of me that is the way that it is because of experiences that I had years ago, e.g. in childhood or in adolescence? And are you still blaming childhood and adolescence for who you are now? "Who is the real me" you should ask? "Can I get back to being that person or is it too late to change now?" "Do I need to in order to be creating the right beliefs?" This raises all sorts of questions—and for me it was a vicious circle and I didn't know where to start in the end. "Did my childhood experiences form me or did I form them?" What came first—the chicken or the egg?

So while it is simple to say "let's form new beliefs" we need to be sure just which part of us is in control of making these new beliefs. A certain amount of self awareness has to occur before you can be free of that doubt.

Division II will prepare you for making the necessary changes. It will give you the necessary insights. Be patient at this point and continue to read. There is more of the picture to be understood before you can start work on yourself.

2.5   REALITY IS SUBJECTIVE

Beliefs have no meaning until you give them meaning. Until then they are just thoughts that you believe in. Let's assume that we all have the same experience at the same time—we are in a cinema watching a movie. When we leave the cinema will we all have had the same experience of that movie? No. Each of us has a different belief structure. A structure that we have flavored by applying the morals of right and wrong, e.g. in the movie, one of us believes that the person was wrong in having killed the other person, but another in the audience thinks that they were right in having done so. Each has their own reasons for their point of view. Each has a personal (or what is called subjective) belief about right and wrong. Neither is right nor wrong. They are just points of view based on beliefs. The point of view is not an objective one. There is no empirical test that can be applied. And even then who is to say that the empirical test was right? The most that can be hoped for is a consensus of opinion and based on that the majority of the audience will determine the success or failure of the movie at the box office. It's all just personal opinion. But some people place a lot of their credibility or image of who they are on their subjective opinions. And they will fight to preserve those points of view as being the "right" points of view. It is the essence of who they think they are. Often they will feel under attack if their beliefs are challenged because they think they are their beliefs. They have become so aligned with them. They don't realize that their beliefs are only their beliefs. So the world you see out there is only the world that you believe that you are seeing. The person standing next to you in the super market line could be seeing a different world to you.

So in this explanation of understanding reality creation, can you see that what you experience is really only experienced from your own point of view and that it is only what you think it is? So if you want to live in a different world or have a different experience why not change the way you think and believe?

Until the thought is judged, analyzed and labeled it means nothing. By definition it can't. It can be explained in terms of physics but it has no meaning as such otherwise. At what instant in time does the kitten become a cat? Subjectivity adds color to the science of life. We give everything meaning. Why do you think schools, governments and religions want to control your Minds? By being aware of how you think you get to make the type of world or person out of you that you want to. It is time to become responsible for your own thoughts, e.g. TV can be a drug that puts the Mind to sleep and stops your having free thoughts. It will even put thoughts into your head, show you the experience that the actors are having and then teach you the so-called truth. If you have already stopped thinking for yourself then it will keep you stupefied. It acts to stop you thinking so that you just absorb everything that it gives you.

Let's go back to our simple example of the day on which it is raining when you get up. You had expected it to be a sunny day. Your initial reaction maybe that it is a lousy, awful, hideous day. If that is your belief then that will be your experience. Obviously the truth is that it is not a lousy, awful, hideous day but in truth merely a day during which it is raining. That fact that you think that it is a lousy, awful, hideous day colors your experience of the day from putting you perhaps into a bad mood (whatever bad may be for you) to otherwise dealing with it in such a way that you would deal with a day on which it rained—dress sensibly, stay indoors etc. On the other hand for example, say I wake up and see that it is a day on which it is raining. Big deal. It is still a fabulous day. You are still alive. You still have your health. It is another day on which to be a SUCCESS. The weather doesn't impact me and slow me down. It is just a wet day. Nothing more. Nothing less. The day is what you think it is. All of life is the same. Reality is what you think it is. Remove the judgment and just let the person, event or thing be what they are. Whenever you argue with what is—whenever you argue with your reality—you suffer. OK. This is one of the most important things I say in this book. Whenever you want something that you are experiencing to be different from what it is then you suffer. Let your reality be what it is. The person, event or thing is as it should be—it is perfect—how do you know? Because it is. If then you want to change it you are free to do that. But you must firstly accept it for what it is first.

2.6   REALITY IS YOUR RESPONSIBILITY

If you choose your beliefs and give your reality its meaning then we have to say that you are responsible for what happens to you. You can't blame someone else. Even if it looks like it that other person, event or thing is doing it to you.

In metaphysics we say that you create your own reality which means that you are responsible for everything that happens to you. Everything. It is your choice—even the time and place of your death. It is your life. It is your reality. You are responsible for what you do and for what happens to you. Taking responsibility means that you can no longer blame. If "all those people out there" (i.e. there's usually more than one person) are "doing it" to you (whatever that "doing it" is) have you stopped to consider for a moment that as you are always the constant in the equation, that perhaps it is you who is doing the doing? That you are the one who should be taking the responsibility for what is happening? "Why does it always happen to me?" can be answered by saying—"because you are doing it to yourself".

This is an exceptionally freeing and liberating approach because now you get to make the life you want; but more than that, you are no longer at the effect of what is going on around you. You don't have to be impacted upon by those that you would otherwise and previously have blamed. Mankind has been living according to the old physics law of Newton's cause and effect. You now need to consciously put yourself at cause. You always were at cause of course but you just weren't quite aware of it. You have been creating your reality by being at the effect of other people, events and things. Your beliefs were creating experiences but you didn't know that. You thought it was the other way around. Swing the pendulum back. It keeps you in polarity but at least you're in control this way. Then you've seen both sides of cause and effect and can understand that Love can come in and lift you out of the polarity. For that matter Love can come at any time and lift you out of it but if you're not open to it or have blocking beliefs then it's hard to let it in. Hence the need for Division II to explain the second half of the big picture. Then Division III shows you how to clear yourself to let in Love that you need in order to create a better life.

Being in control of your life is what matters. It is about taking responsibility for everything that happens to you. Only then will you be free of what happens to you by chance, bad luck, out of your control and from the impact that other people have on you.

Look at someone's life and see what their beliefs must be for them to have that life. It's all waiting for you now. It's your turn. Life is what you make it. It is now time for you to blossom and to be happy and to be at peace.

2.7   MASTERY

The bottom line of you creating your own reality is you becoming a master of your domain. You recognizing that you create it all. No exceptions. This allows you to take back your power from everything. As a master you recognize that you have impact on other people and are responsible for your actions. A master is not caught in the snare of a negatively limiting Ego. They do not judge and knowing their self worth do not need to prove their worth by comparison to others. They are fluent in their being and doing energy, using each as they need to, imagining and creating. This type of energy I talk about in the next chapter.

In Chapter 6.1 on Ego you will come to see that the Ego is merely an interface between your thoughts and your reality. You will realize that your Ego is using your beliefs to manipulate you and your sense of what you think your reality is. So it is better not to start forming new beliefs until you are sure that they are not being created by your Negative Ego.

In later chapters you will also see that your thoughts are coming from a place over which you have, and can have, no control. So how can you ever be in control of what happens to you? By taking mastery over your Ego and then allowing your thoughts to come and go. In that process you have a choice. How do you exercise that? How do you create your own reality?

2.8   THE RAW MATERIALS OF REALITY CREATION

So how do you use the power of thought and feeling to create your reality? There are 3 tools that you need to use.

1.   **Imagination**. Before you can have anything you have to imagine what it is that you want. This is the original thought. An active imagination and a strong will work harmoniously together by feeding each other. This book will help you to find out which part of you is doing the imagining and it will then help you to imagine from the part of you that best serves your higher good—you Higher Self. The aspect of you that is closest to perfection; where there is no pain or suffering—just happiness and peace. I imagine that most people are imagining what they want from the aspect of their Egoic self. That is why there is Fear and pain in your lives.

2.   **Desire**—this is the key to reality creation. This is where the energy comes from. Feel it throughout your body but do not become desperately reliant on what it is that you want. Desire is a feeling that evokes enthusiasm and enlivens the senses. Desire breaks down stagnancy. Stagnancy kills. Use your feelings to fuel your imagination. You have to want to have what you imagine. And that desire can be fueled by Anger, joy, grief, or any other emotion if it is felt strongly enough. The more you feel strongly, the greater the likelihood of those thoughts being experienced. Too much desire though creates

suffering. The suffering usually manifests from you wanting your reality to be different, e.g. impatience leads to suffering. It is a form of non acceptance. Remember that you can't argue with reality. What is, is. Too much thinking about what you want will ensure that it doesn't happen. The reason is because you have stopped living in the moment. Your thoughts have gone to the future and are thinking about what may be. Fear and its cousin, doubt, live in the future. Go there and that is what you will create instead because that is where your thoughts are. If you would think of your dream as a soufflé, then too much thinking will weigh it down and you'll not get a soufflé when the time is up but something else that has the ingredients but not the finesse of a soufflé—perhaps even a pan cake. It's better not to hang out in fantasy land anyway (i.e. the future) but to be real and to stay in the present moment. Feel your desire now then move on with your life.

Why do some people have car accidents and others don't? Why do some people get HIV and die from AIDS and others don't. And what of those who are now in FEAR that they might? So if Fear is an emotion and emotions fuel thoughts and thoughts create reality, then the more you think about something happening to you and the more you feel it then the more likely it is that that something will manifest. Thinking+Feeling=Your Reality Creation. Again it comes down to the question: what part of you is doing the imagining? Your Ego that devours, craves and relishes Fear for its sustenance or your Higher Self which sustains in Love and lives in peace and happiness?

3   All of that is positive thinking and people do it all the time. But it doesn't work all the time does it? Why? One reason is conflicting beliefs and living in the future or the past in your Mind. The other is that you are missing the secret ingredient of **Expectancy**. A real expectancy, knowing or trusting that you will receive what it is that you want. The more you hang out with your Higher Self and in states of Love the more you will

come to trust and expect to receive what it is that the Real You imagines and desires. In those cases you will be in tune with your creative possibilities. All of this will become clearer as I explain how reality works.

2.9   THE TOOLS WITH WHICH TO BUILD REALITY

You create your own reality by using certain basic tools and raw materials. You need to ensure that these are clean (Division III will show you how). If not you will prepare a reality that is not exactly what you want, e.g. if your thoughts are tinged with Anger then your reality will be angry around the edges too. Your present reality will give you clues as to whether or not things are going right. You'll know. Just remember to check which aspect of you that wants the changes. Is it your Ego, your Shadow or your Higher Self or is it coming from emotional blockages, e.g. Victimhood or Martryhood? (Chapter 5 explains these).

1.   **THOUGHTS AND FEELINGS.** Feelings are really only unexpressed thoughts. You need to be aware of what you are thinking. Many of us daydream. Our thoughts wander aimlessly following down paths of fantasy which we indulge. These thoughts are the soil from which our reality grows. Be careful what you think. There is a fine line between thinking and believing. And an even finer line between believing and desiring. Before you know it, you have got caught up thinking the same thing over and again, mulling it over, playing with it, feeling it, believing it and almost tasting it. This is how realities form. There's an old saying—"be careful for what you ask for because you may get it."

2.   **BELIEFS AND ATTITUDES.** These come from the thoughts and feelings. As an exercise write down your beliefs. I have explained earlier how to recognize them. Your reality will tell you. Your experience is a result of your beliefs and attitudes.

Beliefs can't be changed. That is an old concept that does not work. You can only accept the beliefs that you have and create new ones.

3. **CHOICES AND DECISIONS.** Because the thoughts and beliefs are yours so too then is the reality that is created from them. As it is therefore your reality you have a choice as to what you can or can't do. You are never trapped in your reality. Whenever you do something then, consciously say to your self "I now choose to…" If you take this action you will always be reminded that you took the action and this will start moving you out of the state of mind of being a Victim or Martyr or from being stuck in Guilt. You won't be able to blame anyone for what happens to you. This may make you angry at first because now you have no one to blame but yourself and after years of blaming it may not be comfortable to know that you have been doing this to yourself all along. Sadness may also arise at the thought of how much you have hurt yourself. Be gentle with yourself. No one had ever taught you how to create reality and you are not to blame. Eventually you will be much more careful with what you think. You will learn to recognize the emotional blockages the instant they arise and when you are coming from Ego or your Shadow is playing itself out. Little by little you will learn to manage these origins of thought until finally you are at peace. The punishing thoughts will fall away almost completely and in some cases completely. Creating from this state of mind makes for a peaceful and still reality. If all aspects of you are quite and at peace so too will your world be. Your reality is a reflection of your thoughts. Having made your choices you can then make decisions. Ask yourself the following questions—

    1.   What do I want now?
    2.   What is my motivation for wanting it?
    3.   Why don't I want it?
    4.   What am I afraid of it I was to get what I want? Would I be punished? Would someone stop loving me?

Chapter 3

—MALE AND FEMALE ENERGY

3.1 THE METAPHYSICS OF MALE AND FEMALE ENERGY

Really there is just energy (and even that is just a thought that helps us make sense of the world). For the purpose of understanding the polarity that we think the world is, energy can be divided into the polarities of male and female energy.

The following table is based on Polarity and when these are joined together lead to Oneness or Wholesomeness—a merging of both aspects.

THE MALE ENERGY	THE FEMALE ENERGY
Represented by **KNOWLEDGE**	Represented by **LOVE** (the glue that holds the Universe together)
Called Light or **FORM**	Called **CONTENT**
It is the energy of **DOING**	It is the energy of **BEING**
Characterized by **WILLING, ACTING** and **THINKING**	Characterized by **FEELING**
It dynamically **CREATES** and puts into action. His joy comes from creating her dream. He thrives on it.	It allows perception to conception. She is **IMAGINATION** itself.
Recognized by Self Reliance and Follow Through, Focusing Thought on what is wanted.	Recognized by the attributes of **GIVING** and **RECEIVING** and of **NURTURING** and being nurtured, of being made with Love.
The energy of **GOD**	The energy of the **GODDESS**
Creation is by using energy to create Form. The form is then there for the Content to fill it, e.g. building an art gallery is being male but the paintings – the art and the feeling they represent—are female. The World says that you should be male and do.	Creation is by gathering Content to force Form into existence, e.g. you collect the art works and design the building around them so as to show them off in their best light. Because female is passive it is seen as being weaker but this is not true. It is as strong as male and leads to even more inventive creating.
It is the shaping, focusing and forming energy; refocusing and reforming to create something new.	She is able. Her ability is to give the impetus that allows you to perform.
His motivation is to seek and to search for meaning.	Her motivation is the willingness to achieve.
He is the protector, her warrior.	She is here to balance all things to be in their place.

Traditionally men have been in touch with and displayed more male energy and similarly with women and their domain over the female energy. So it is a convenient way to describe energy this way—he works and she sits at home (or so the male based mythology would have us believe—we know that she never "sat"). There has always been the so-called "war of the sexes". Understanding polarity will explain why. The war came about because the male gender denied his female energy and the female gender denied her male side. And no it wasn't that the male was dominating the female. She agreed to it. It was a choice. This is a planet of free will. So now after thousands of years of male domination the pendulum is swinging back the other way toward female energy influence in reality creation. Little wonder as to why men are feeling threatened, as their territory is lost "to the other side". Men are territorial and fight for land. Little wonder there is confusion on who should be doing what. The goal posts are moving and the rules are changing—it has become a free for all. The boundaries are disappearing and there is uncertainty as to the roles being played by men and women. And everyone of us is the umpire in this new game of life. The "war of the sexes" didn't exist in those relationships where Love was the basis of the relationship. This energy let the polarities balance and there was no conflict between the male trying to dominate and the female trying to manipulate. These distorted male and female attributes only arose where one or the other of the people in the equation was denying the other polarity within them. In those cases the partner or spouse played out the denied polarity and this in turn "pressed the buttons" of the person in denial. More on that later in this chapter when I describe distorted male and female energy and later in Chapter 6.3 on the Shadow. Once you understand how they energies are just polarities you begin to understand how the world really works.

Do not confuse these energies as being gender reliant. Everyone of us carries both energies. We all have the potential to imagine and to create, to do and to be, to think and to feel. It is just a matter of accessing those energies. And that is by intention and practice. It is a skill and can be learned. There are plenty of "how to" books out there to teach you these skills and on how to access your own energy. You move between them as you would move your fingers up and down a piano keyboard. Sometimes playing imagination and then letting yourself create your dream. In so doing you create a beautiful song— a harmony or resonance of energy that attracts your reality to you through your thoughts, beliefs, choices and decisions.

The tradition of only men doing and thinking and of only women imagining and feeling is changing. We as a humanity are beginning to free ourselves from our self-imposed definitions of what a man is supposed to be and of what a woman is supposed to be. In so doing we free ourselves to access more of the energy of the opposite polarity that we have previously denied ourselves from having.

People are learning to access the energy of the opposite polarity from within themselves—where it was all along. The old way taught that the world existed outside you—so logically if you wanted something you looked outside of you in the outside world for evidence of it. We were unaware that if we believed that it existed then that projected belief would lead us to finding the evidence that we sought. Because our behavior was so socially controlled we strongly looked to the opposite gender to fulfill our need for internal balance. There were plenty of other reasons too—like sex, protection, survival, political manipulation and all the reason why any person does anything—but I am talking on a much deeper spiritual and psychological level. The New World says that the outside world comes from within you—so the place to look for fulfillment is inside you. Your outside reality will give you the clues as to your beliefs but that is all they are—clues. Have you noticed how insular and isolated people are becoming today as they become more reliant on technology and look outwards for their answers? This is why Love is now more important than ever. To heal the polarity and to fill the emptiness and pain that the conflict of polarity creates. A conflict that will become more painful the more you buy into an outside reality. What is needed on the planet to heal it and everyone in it is a new paradigm. A totally new mind set. The old one of male domination isn't working. Metaphysics is such a set and this is why millions of people are turning to it to give them the answers that they have known all along but which humanity forgot hundreds of years ago. We need to move away from the male energy reality and by accessing the female energy go into Oneness and balance. Harmony and peace within ourselves.

Part of the male-female attraction on an energy level has been to balance the polarities of those energies. Part of the attraction was to create a space where we could see ourselves—both the conscious and denied aspects—reflected back to us through our beliefs by the behavior of our partner/spouse. That function of a relationship won't change. Now we are freer to have more relationships, and not just sexual ones, but partnerships of a de-facto type where marriage isn't deemed to be necessary. Of relationships at work and socially, which take on new meaning in supporting us emotionally, in place of the extended family network that previously supported us but which began to disappear after the 1960's in that time of social revolution and growth in personal awareness. Being more self reliant we now do not need the member of the opposite gender so much to give us what we are finding inside us. We still have all the other reasons though (like sex, protection, survival, political manipulation and all the reason why any person does anything).

The social boundaries that separated males and females and kept them separate are well on the way to being demolished, so as to permit each gender to cross over to the other, at will, to access the energy of the other. The Women's Movement, which flowered in the early 20th Century, was part of this. WW2 and the Social Revolution of the "60s were others. The freedom of the 1960's taught people to Love everyone and not to judge them. The continuing Gay & Feminist Movements are the most current form of this global shift in consciousness.

Thanks to women and homosexuals taking back their power and their rights and accepting themselves we have

anti-discrimination and equal opportunity legislation (they themselves being a result of a changing consciousness and not the cause of it, i.e. these changes are in fact the physical manifestation of the changes that have already occurred in the beliefs of the people). Gender and sexuality therefore are becoming non-issues. Which is great because now we can look past them to the true underlying philosophies that they represent.

Being homosexual and/or feminist in the late 20th Century was really all about learning to break out of the chains of social conformity that kept us all locked into an age-old male-female energy polarity. A polarity where we couldn't be all of who we really were and one where we would punish ourselves for not being all of who we were. It was a beacon showing us new ways of expressing personal freedom and a bridge of self discovery that let us balance ourselves. It was women and the homosexuals who had the desire to change society not because of what they thought—but because of what they felt—and in so doing let us all see the potential and strength that awaited us in our internal reunion. The Gay Rights Movement and Feminism are the greatest social changes to have occurred in human history. They go to the very heart of society itself, the very essence of what determines how society functions. They are a prime example of how belief backed by desire will create a new reality. One which reflects the truth of the person creating the reality.

Gender is becoming irrelevant to task and performance of function. Already this is evident as the sexes cross over and borrow from the physical stereotype of the other—men with earrings and long hair, women with shaved heads and work boots. The barriers of gender are breaking down.

Women have always been allowed to express their Love of one another both physically and emotionally. Men had encouraged this as a purely sexual experience for themselves. Lesbians and the Feminist Movement have let women take back their power from the male energy allowing women to move into the male domain of business, the professions, government, manufacturing, design and even space travel. Resistance to them is still felt in the most conservative quarter—the Church. Its male dominated hierarchy has overseen the domination of this planet by male energy for eons. And it has the most to loose. God will have been toppled if a woman were to become Pope for God has always been seen as being a man and man as being a reflection of God. This gender specific terminology of God is old fashioned and out of date. It needs to be re-visited and over-hauled.

Men are now accessing their female polarities without having to bond emotionally with women in order to access their female energy and the same is true vice versa with women. Homosexuals have taught men and women that it is OK to do this.

Generally speaking gay men feel a lacking of male energy and seek the male energy from other males to compensate for it. The gay males display too little of the traits commonly associated with a male, and attraction is based on balancing out the energy with someone who is the opposite of them or the same as them.

Generally speaking it is the same with lesbians only they seek the female energy as they have too much of the male energy. This is only one of the reasons behind homosexuality. Many seek the Love that they feel that they didn't get from other members of their own sex when they were children. For each of them though the reason is different. I believe that the bottom line is that they are attracted to members of their own sex from a desire to be fulfilled by an energy that they have insufficient of themselves. They identify this energy that they are lacking with the gender that is traditionally associated with that energy and seek a relationship with it. This is no more than what heterosexuals do in their quest for completion. As the lines between what is male and what is female continue to blur, it will not be inconceivable to find more and more people experimenting with any combination of genders in their relationships. Perhaps even to the point where the labels come off sexual orientation and a more sexually ambiguous or androgynous person evolves. Gender will cease to be relevant as an issue.

Gay men taught men that it is OK to take pride in appearance and to be attractive on a physical level. In the beginning it was women who accepted gay men. They recognized in the gay man the sensitivity, the being in touch with feeling and all those other female energy traits, that they possessed. And gay men weren't sexual predators of women, so they felt safe with them. There was plenty to have in common too—they both liked men and each group appreciated imagination in creativity.

Males were terrified of gay men sexually pursuing them—it was too much of a threat to their identity to be vulnerable and to submit to another man in the way that a man demands of a woman. In other words they were feeling like a lot of women felt when treated as sex objects—and they didn't like it. When men start accessing their female energy and start loving one another there can't by definition be war. Love balances the polarity. This is why Love is so frightening to men. They will have to let go of their identities as warriors. Not warriors in the sense of being the "Good Knight" fighting for honor but as war-like beings that kill to control. They will have to learn not to dominate and can do so by accessing their female energy.

But being driven to be with women, and seeing that the gay men were getting all the attention, men began to imitate the looks of gay men—in clothing, taste, presentation and life style. They learned that women like men who are groomed, pretty, well built, who appreciate the arts, are beautiful and aren't afraid to express their creative talents. Consequently, the stereotype of the rough and tough man, the protector who fights for the woman before ravishing her, is changing. That was a hard one for men to live up to. Little wonder gay life became so attractive. It is the ultimate men's club. No wonder the conservative White Anglo Saxon Protestants (WASPS) were so threatened by this new competition. This threat to their dominance and control over the world. As heterosexual men mixed with gay men, they learned that there was nothing to fear from being in touch with their own feelings and they learned to accept their own energy both male and female. In turn this led to acceptance of the gay culture. So much so that in early 2000 someone like Corey Johnson a senior at Masconomet High in Topsfield, Mass., can be captain of the high school football team and come out to the total acceptance of his team mates. Rick Reilly a journalist at Sports Illustrated in its column was able to say "maybe we're actually getting somewhere in the U.S.A. A young man who leads young men comes out as gay, and it makes such a ruckus you can still hear the crickets chirp." In fact the football team received an award from the Lesbian and Straight Education Network for tolerance! What's going on when a bastion of male competition isn't threatened by non-traditional forms of Love? The answer is that Fear is no longer present. These incidents are small—even tiny—but they underscore a massive social change that is occurring in the world. Love is seeping through.

Similarly with women—although women have traditionally been more open to Love. Their greatest Fear has been of the untamed male. He is becoming less common in this new age of gender bending.

As a result, we have seen the emergence of the S.N.A.G. (the Sensitive New Age Guy). There's a very good Australian comedy play called S.N.A.G. which shows the life of a man in the new age. Here all the rules of relationship and behavior have changed and the women have taken back their power. It deals with the SNAG's divorce when he finds his wife in bed with his sister and how he has to come to learn to get in touch with his feelings and to express them.

The house-husband is an extension of this new role for the male gender. A complete reversal of roles. You see them in supermarkets with the baby in the stroller where once the supermarket was the domain of women. Traditionally the woman went to market while the man was in the fields toiling. In male dominated societies like Portugal this is still the case. Where ever you find a highly freed and expressive male and female population you will find a freed gay population. It is no longer shameful for a man to stay at home and the principal bread winner to be a female. She could even be an Executive—that representation of the pinnacle of power previously only held by a man. The sexes are becoming independent of each other.

So it was the women who were leading the men around. As is the case in metaphysics—imagination leads creativity. Being leads doing. It is not women as such who are doing this—but the female energy as played out by women. All the behavior of the 1960s to now has been an analogy for the development, movement and inter-action of male and female energy. That is all that has been happening.

The importance of Love has re-emerged, especially regarding the old belief that Love had to be earned and was the sole domain of heterosexuals. The stigma of same sex relationships is going as people realize that Love is not gender reliant and that everyone deserves and needs Love.

So the explanation is here. The benefits to humanity are becoming obvious. A whole new chapter is opening up. The world is becoming a better place. On one level there is now so much less pain and suffering as people are free to be not only who they are but to grow into being more of who they are. So in this shifting energy you can see how it has affected changes.

But there is still resistance to these ongoing and unstoppable shifts. Some people who previously felt safe in the unchanging conditions of the '50s, 60's and even the early 70's (they are mainly in the over 50 age bracket now or come from Conservative families) can't understand why these dramatic social changes happened. The new behavior challenges their being and identity and they don't like it.

For some, they no longer know how they are supposed to act. They don't know what it is like to be a man or to be a woman. Life was so much less complicated before. They are used to being told what to do within a rigid framework of church, school and state, basing their beliefs on teachings that have been literally translated rather than figuratively interpreted and without regard for the effects of time on change itself. They do not understand freedom or the responsibility that freedom brings. This freedom to them is confronting. They don't know what is right and what is wrong any more. There is no such thing as right and wrong on one level anyway (everything is just subjective belief). All the rules have been broken and often discarded completely. So they retreat to the past for their answers while trying to control the present. They seek to stop change before they are completely lost. This they do by trying to stop those effecting the changes.

You can't turn back the clock. As a humanity we are evolving into a New World and this movement can't be stopped. It began hundreds of years ago, slowly at first as people began to free themselves from the control of their feudal kings and lords. Then down through bloody revolutions, French, American and Russian, over throwing the aristocracy and past tyrants, we are now to be free of the limiting beliefs so that we can now see the secrets of reality creation itself. Finally we are beginning to experience freedom from the false self— the Ego, from conformity and society itself. Ultimately and sufficiently free and responsible to create our own reality. The end of this long journey is literally at hand. While we engage in the world of polarity there will always be the conservatives and the radicals and the pain that comes from conflict. These people need Love more than most.

And the male homosexuals suffered as well. In their fight for recognition in the face of all of society, they were savagely opposed by the institution of the church that saw it as an abomination in the sight of God. Governments imposed a statutory banning on the practice and rigidly, and at times gleefully, entrapped people by that law. The medical practice considered the practice to be a deviant disorder treatable by shocking practice and peer pressure. Ostracization from families often meant that the gay male found himself living in a gay ghetto trying to forget his own inner pain in a cocktail of drugs, alcohol and promiscuous sex. He was fearful and on guard from societal attack and had a belief system of low Self Esteem, which had been learned from society, school and church. Within a few years of being "out of the closet" this emotional and psychological toll left the gay male living in a flight or fight reality. It looked fabulous on the outside but the lifestyle created stresses and these created toxins which weakened their bodies eventually manifesting as a disease which reflected their underlying belief that they were under attack from their environment. That disease was called AIDS, and acted on the ill person by attacking his immune defenses to the world around him. As a result of that he eventually died from things as simple as the air he breathed—and many thousands of young men died literally fighting by example for the right to Love whoever they choose to and to be free to express who they were. It was another battle in the long fight for freedom. A suicide mission for some perhaps but a mission all the same. Their deaths and the resulting grief of parents and friends and Lovers from losing such young lives opened the hearts of men and women everywhere to compassion and acceptance and allowed a great flooding of Love onto the planet to heal it and to further raise evolutionary consciousness.

By definition an approach that tries to control and keep the past intact must fail. Everything is changing all the time. Energy must keep moving. It is inherent in what energy is. You only have the now. The past is gone. The future is an illusion. The solution is to allow what is. To not deny your reality. If you don't then you will suffer. And the time for suffering is over.

You have all heard of left brained and right brained. The logical side of the brain and the creative side and how people function in the world using these hemispheres. This explanation for the working of the brain is based on the philosophy of polarity. Each side can be compared to the functions of male and female energy. The stereotype is that he thinks logically and she imagines and is artistic. He creates by putting pen to paper. She envisions through her senses. Energy is not gender specific but has been labeled so and in so doing has limited the growth of the person's beliefs about themselves and therefore their experience. If you want to learn which side of your brain is more dominant and whether you are a visual or an auditory learner there is a great little computer test put together by the US firm, Synergistic Learning Incorporated. Contact them for details.

3.2   DISTORTED MALE ENERGY—FEMALE ENERGY

The male and female energy of most people is out of balance. That is one of the causes of disease. Here are the characteristics of distorted energy and how they manifest—

DISTORTED MALE	DISTORTED FEMALE
Represented by characteristics of wanting to **CONTROL**. This comes from Ego and is often demonstrated as Anger.	Represented by characteristics of **WORTHLESSNESS**.
Found where there is either too much male energy or the female energy has been denied.	Found where there is either too much female energy or the male energy has been denied.
It occupies a position of **CHAUVINISM**. Putting a male in the superior position.	She **HATES MEN** seeing them as bullies, horrible, aggressive and nasty.
He creates a reality of **FORM** with no content. Looks wonderful but it's hollow and empty and no heart.	Life is all **CONTENT** and no form. She has no way of putting her ideas into form. She's 'up in the air' and unpractical.
Carries **SUPPRESSED EMOTION** and becomes a human machine working relentlessly, doing more, getting more but never stopping to feel.	**HARBORS NEGATIVE EMOTION.** Blame, Anger, resentment and won't forgive. This festers away causing disease.
He is **IMPRISONED** by an **IMAGE** of what he wants or of how reality works. He is rigid, e.g. I'm a man and you are a woman so you have to behave a certain way.	She experiences **STAGNATION** of her **DREAMS** with unfinished fantasies and delusions of success. As the positive of this trait is imagination then the negative is that her dreams become nightmares.
He exercises **DOMINATION** and holds the belief of having to control so as not to be controlled. He strives for perfection in order to gain approval and avoid punishment. "Teach me the rules and I'll be perfect. And when I'm perfect I will deserve Love". This **COMPETITION** leads him to judgment of others and all else and this judgment separates him from that which he is seeking.	She rules by **MANIPULATION**. There is a destructive over emphasis of male energy at the expense of the female energy. This is **LOWER SELF** behavior and exhibits as spite, hate, hurt and jealousy just for the sake of it.

He is **TOTALLY ALIENATED** from the World and is in a state of not belonging.	She is in a state of **FUNCTIONING IN POTENTIAL** and not of actualizing. She's always in the future and being ungrounded never achieves anything. She lives in a state of mind of "If only ... then .... " Her view of herself is one of worthlessness. She actively operates **CONTROL** and covertly **MANIPULATES**.
Caught in active **SELF PITY** he becomes a Victim.	Her actions culminate in her not doing and she ends up in **STAGNANCY** denying and destroying herself passively becoming a Victim and Martyr, self destructing and particularly susceptible to cancer and AIDS.

Without Love there is Fear and terror, panic and chaos. When Anger emerges we deny the female and chauvinism begins. Anger therefore is separation from Love. Every issue goes to a lack of Love. One role of the female is to nourish. With her Love the male goes forward to be more of who he is. When the male becomes angry the female closes down and goes into Fear believing that she now has to manipulate rather than inspire. She becomes untrusting and greedy never being satisfied. Insatiable. In response he now has to prove that he is good enough to be loved. The cycle goes on infinitely. The female demands more. The man continues to prove. The male becomes exhausted and dies. Do you think that distorted male and female energy affects our longevity? And can you see how it could be a cause for disease? Does this scenario remind you of "the battle of the sexes"? Can you see any reason for wanting to have distorted male or female energy?

3.3   THE IMPACT OF MALE & FEMALE ENERGY

The bottom line therefore in metaphysics and the most important thing that I will say in this book is that **you create your own reality** by either—

1   **choosing** to cause it (i.e. being active and doing something about it—using the male energy) or

2   **allowing** others (either in physical form or aspects of your Unconscious self) to cause it for you (i.e. letting it happen— using the female energy) and by doing so using the tools and raw materials of manifestation that I have described in the previous chapter.

This philosophy is now being taught at post graduate level in the communication syllabus as an explanation of how meaning in our world is created. Next it will be taught at under graduate level, then high school level, then primary school level and eventually it will be the dominant belief system in the western world. Parents will teach children. The medium of film and television will teach society. Quantum physics and science are beginning to support this. Religion (faith) and science are re-merging. This trend is becoming obvious now as New Age principles are being taught by parents and even television in the day to day existence that we all share.

Metaphysics is becoming main stream. Already millions of people in the western world have adopted this philosophy as the basis of their lives—certainly anyone who did est, Forum, Insight, Stuart Wilde, Tony Robbins, Caroline Myss and any of the other great speakers of today. Not to forget the multitude of other self awareness and positive thinking workshops that have been taught in the last 30 years and are taught on a weekly basis throughout the western world. All say that you create your own reality. So you have to be responsible for what happens to you which means you have to stop playing Victim by blaming other people for what happens to you. Sure other people have impact but you choose your reaction. This is an important distinction to remember.

DIVISION II

—WHO ARE YOU?

Chapter 4

4.1 INTRODUCTION

You now know that you create your own reality. You now understand how the outside world is created. That's half the big picture. You are the second half. But who are you? At the center of your world is you. You are the only constant in your life. You are everywhere that you go. So you need to know who you are before you can understand how you affect what is going on in your world. So the question that I want you to consider while reading this Division is—who are "you?" By asking yourself "who am I?" will begin to trigger the response. Ask yourself this question three or four times before reading further, think about it and then sit quietly for a moment and see what answers come. And if you come up with an illogical answer, don't let your logical Mind convince you that your illogical answer is wrong. You are not what you seem. You are so much more and at the same time you are so much less. Finding out who you are is what this Division is all about. Then once you know that and how you impact on your world you can start changing it for the better.

We all know how the body works—chemistry, molecular structure, the workings of vitamins, amino acids, DNA, the nervous and immune systems and everything else that makes us what is tangible in the world that we can see. We all understand basically how the body works. It needs fuel, it expels waste, it moves, its self-driven, it communicates, it thinks, it feels, it wears out and dies or in some cases just fades away. This is the model that we have been conditioned to believe. This is a mass conscious belief. The beliefs of the mass conscious are held in the Unconscious Mind. A place where we are not aware of what beliefs exist. If we were aware then we would have a conscious awareness of them.

The understanding of the human body is based on Newton's Laws—that man is a machine and that we live in a mechanistic world. This model sees the body as a complex machine controlled by the brain. To traditional western medicine everything is mechanical. The heart is a pump. The kidney a filter. Surgeons are really only high tech bio-plumbers—interrupting the system to take out the rust or the blockage, installing new piping or a pump or a filter and then reconnecting the whole system. Magic bullets (or drugs) have been designed to hit a target that is causing a problem. And this approach is very useful and in many cases a necessary ingredient in the healing process.

But the body is much more than what we see as we shall now discover. It is also the energy that we can't see which surrounds the body. In fact the physical body derives from these fields of energy. It is not the other way around. This is a new concept here in the West. This energy that circles the body is in layers, each layer having a different purpose in influencing and creating the physical body. These range from instigating and controlling cellular growth (the Etheric Body and the Chakra System—this is the system which provides the means for the energy of the Etheric, Astral (Emotional), Mental and Causal Bodies to form the physical body via energy portals—see chapter 4.2 and 4.3), the energies of the Astral (Emotional) Body (Chapter 5) and the conception of ideas and making them happen in your life (the Mental Body—Chapter 6). This Division looks at these energy bodies and a field of energy greater than all of them—Consciousness itself (the Causal Body—Chapter 7).

The resonance of each of the energy bodies rises in frequency the further it travels away from the physical body. Eventually the outer field of energy becomes indiscernible from the physical body and merges with all other energy in the Universe. This largest field of energy we call the Universe, Consciousness, the Source, the Isness, All

That Is, the Force, the main frame computer, Universal Consciousness or just simply God. In this book I will call it the Universe.

By the end of this Division you will see that the body and the energy fields around it are one and the same. All experience is stored in the body (not the brain). The body is the product of its experience and the beliefs that have produced that experience. Memory is actually stored at a cellular level in the membranes (memory-brains). So all healing has to occur at all the energy levels that make up the body and its energy fields and not just on the physical level. You can't heal half the body, you have to heal it all and because it is an inter-connected organism you have to treat it as such.

Traditionally, Western Medicine just treats the physical body while seeing beliefs and emotions as only partly, if at all, related to the illness. That is changing though. Eastern medicine though deals much more with the unseen aspects of the body—the energy that the body derives from. When the polarities of Eastern and Western medicine merge there will be more than a balance. A synergy will exist that is much bigger than anyone of us can imagine now. May I suggest that it is only with the overlaying of the metaphysical model that a more complete understanding can be achieved of the entire Energy System that is us and what is also called the Mind-Body. Throughout this book though I will keep referring to you as an Energy System because that is what you are. All energy—some solid some not.

So if your physical body is more than physicality and includes fields of energy that reach up to and include the Universe, then who is the "you" that we keep talking about? Can you isolate who you are from your thoughts and feelings? This Division will show you that these are also part of the energy bodies that contribute to your physical body. Who then is it that is doing the thinking and who are you? Ponder this question while you read on.

4.2 THE ETHERIC BODY

Many decades ago Einstein formulated the theories that became known as quantum physics. At the time everyone thought that he was mad. But by the 1940's however as his theories were being proven to be true he was being hailed as a genius—the greatest thinker of the century & one of the greatest of all time. Time Magazine declared him to be "The Person of the Century". The person most influential in directing the entire 20th Century. The century which saw more scientific advancement than of all prior human history combined.

Einstein said that everything in the Universe is energy and only energy—there is nothing else. He proved this when $E=mc^2$ was proved to be correct. Everything in the Universe is an energy field within a larger energy field, which in turn is in a larger energy field, which in turn is in a larger energy field and so on and so forth one inside the other. The electron inside the atom, inside the molecule, inside the cell, inside the bone, inside the body, inside the neighborhood, inside the village, inside the district, inside the County, inside the State, inside the country, inside the continent, inside the planet, inside the atmosphere, inside the solar system, inside the galaxy, inside the Universe.

The Einstein model is based on the understanding that the molecular arrangement of the body is a complex network of interwoven energy fields, i.e. there are more than one. This energetic network or what we'll call your physical body, is organized and nourished by "subtle" energetic systems which co-ordinate life in the body. These energy systems are in a hierarchy and co-ordinate electrophysiologic and hormonal function as well as the cellular structure of the body. This hierarchy is based on the resonance (or frequency) of the energy. The slower that the energy resonates, the more dense the matter becomes, e.g. the resonance of a stone is slower than the resonance of air. Ice is more dense than water because the resonance of the water has been slowed down.

There is now scientific evidence to support the theory of the existence of a human holographic energy field (or what is called the

Etheric Body) which, is a template for the growth, development and repair of the body. So it is now proven that the body is a lot more than just flesh and blood. It has an energy field around it. So the Etheric Body vibrates at a higher resonance than the physical body. It is in fact vibrating so quickly that we can't see it with the naked eye.

It is primarily from these subtle levels that health and illness originates. The energy systems of our body are powerfully affected by our emotions (energy in motion) and level of spiritual balance as well as by nutritional and environmental factors. And our beliefs—what we call "thought energy".

Within this map of energy—called the Etheric Body—is all the information that the physical body needs for cellular growth and repair. This information works in conjunction with the body's genetics. The physical and Etheric bodies are so connected energetically that the physical body can't exist without it. If the Etheric Body becomes distorted the physical body reflects that distortion as disease.

The point at which the physical body meets the Etheric Body is along the acupuncture meridians. These acupuncture points are a microscopic network of ducts. The energy that moves from the energy field to the body is called Chi. When the Chi is disturbed (or goes out of balance) illness can follow—it depends on how severe the disturbance is and for how long it occurs. This starts to explain what acupuncture is and why it works. Science has since gone on to prove why it works.

The life force that sustains us is the energy that comes from our energy systems. No life force=no energy field=no life. If the energy field goes askew then so does the attached molecular/cellular structure, i.e. our bodies. The Chinese call this life force "Chi".

Einstein predicted that the subtle energies travel faster than light. Thought already travels faster than light and in a 5th dimensional reality, thought manifests as reality instantly, e.g. I am on Earth. I think I am on Venus. Instantly I am on Venus. That's a lot faster than light travel! What would the future be like if we all evolved consciously to the 5th Dimension? Think about it because that is where evolutionary consciousness is taking us. Have you noticed how time has been speeding up? That it doesn't take as long any more things to happen after you have thought about them? But what would be the dangers if every thought you had manifested instantly? So you need to learn to channel your thinking and to know who is doing the thinking or you could end up in a mess—especially if your Ego was in control. You see, your Ego is really trying to kill you and Chapter 6 will show you why.

Vitally, Einstein proved that we are made up of the energy of the Universe. In other words we are the Universe. Energy and matter are the same thing—just resonating at different frequencies in different forms—but everything is the same. Therefore everything is connected. We are all one. Movement in one energy system therefore affects through a ripple pattern everything around it and all that is resonating at the same frequency as it. Like waves that a stone makes when thrown into a pond of water. We talk more about this when we get to consciousness. Einstein was on the way to proving the existence of God.

We all know that DNA directs the development of individual cells. Every cell is our body has the master DNA instructions on how to create the body. Holograms work on the same principle as DNA. Within the tiniest part of the hologram is to found the entire blueprint. 98% of all DNA living things have the same DNA. So how amazing must be that extra DNA that we humans have? Holograms are also made out of light. It is now proven that the Etheric Body fills out the cells to make them 3D. That is how we become 3rd dimensional. The 3rd dimension is a space in which form is holographic. Any artist will tell you that we are holograms—that is what 3rd dimensional reality is. The body can be broken down into molecules and atoms. Quantum physics tells us that every atom is more than 99.9999% empty space. Within each atom are sub-atomic particles. At this level all matter is literally frozen light. We are therefore made out of light. For thousands of years metaphysicians have called us Beings of Light. Science has now proved it. We think of ourselves as being solid flesh and blood but scientifically we are holograms of light. The importance of this is that it has been proven that light can be influenced by thought. And we all think. And we know that thought creates reality. So could it be possible that by thinking that we could actually affect our bodies or the world around us? Yes. You've heard of the power of positive thinking. You've heard of mind over matter. Can you imagine the implications of this for healing, for peace, for growth and inventiveness? The potential exists for you to think yourself well. What you think you see, you see. Your beliefs are the power that convinces you. The secret is out. It is now scientifically proven—you do create your own reality. But who is doing the thinking? You?

Machines exist that can prove the existence of the Etheric Body but none exist that can prove the existence of the higher fields of resonance that contribute to causing the body to exist. Radio waves existed before a machine was invented to prove that they were discovered to existed. Then a radio transmitter was invented.

Can you imagine that one day machines will exist that can not only prove the existence of these higher resonances of energy but can in fact create them. Can you imagine a machine that could simulate the frequency of perfect heath for each of the energy bodies. If disease is a frequency out of alignment, then could a machine that corrects the frequency (by raising it back to its perfect pitch) be the 21st Century equivalent to penicillin? And what if this machine could destroy cells in the body that were out of control (say for instance like Cancer cells) by raising the vibration or resonance of the diseased cells so that they exploded or disintegrated—in much the same way as a high C will smash glass or a microwave can destroy cellular structure because their form could not hold the higher vibration. The result would be the elimination of surgery and chemotherapy. This is the potential of a new branch of science called vibrational medicine. The study of the energy fields around the body has the potential to open up totally new avenues of healing that can't yet be imagined.

4.3   THE CHAKRA SYSTEM

As Einstein found, everything in the Universe is energy and this includes your thoughts, feelings and beliefs. Different thoughts and feelings resonate at different frequencies. These thoughts and feelings can be identified and labeled and then it can be shown on which parts of the body they have an effect.

The physical body is "stepped down" energy vibrating slowly enough to form into something solid. We have seen this from our understanding of the Etheric Body and from what you will find in the remainder of this Division.

How are these higher energies transformed and impacted on the person? The portals through which the various energies enter the body are called chakras.

Chakras—an Indian word meaning wheel—are specialized energy centers or portals in the body associated with major nerves and glands in the body. It is these chakras, which act as transformers stepping down the vibration of the energy from the Etheric, Astral (Emotional), Mental and Causal Bodies and making them into hormones, cells, nerves and what you see as being your body and life. The chakras provide the high energy needed for running the physical body. Their secondary role is to then propel that energy back out of the chakras into the outside world— the 3rd Dimension that we call reality, the holographic illusion that is held together by thought energy. In this way the higher vibrations of energy that make you up directly influence your external reality. When chakras are out of balance, spent or impacted they can become weak. If out of balance the incoming energy can be impeded and this can be reflected directly in your reality as that impeded energy is projected to the Outer World to form your reality.

The body functions as a sophisticated motion picture projector. While the motion picture projector is powered by electricity, we are powered by the Light of the Universe—Consciousness (the Causal Body—see Chapter 7). Both have bodies and programs and both project these programs onto a screen. When light is shown through the film reel, the image is projected two dimensionally onto a flat screen in front of you. When light shines through the chakras this is projected three dimensionally onto the inner surface of an imaginary three hundred and sixty degree sphere or bubble in which you stand at the center.

Have you realized yet that you are the common denominator in your reality? I have mentioned this before. You are always everywhere you are. That everything goes on "around you". The program that we see "out there" and which we call our reality, is influenced by our energy bodies. The light that shines through us is the knowledge that is the male energy that I explained in Chapter 3. It is complimented by the female energy.

In both cases the projected image is an illusion. We enjoy the two dimensional image with sight and sound and we do not think it is real because it has no depth of field and we only experience it with limited senses, e.g. you can't taste a movie. It can manipulate and prompt our feelings though and have impact on us. The three dimensional image is no more real just because it is solid or appears to be so, just because we can access it with our five senses. In the movie *The Sixth Sense*, the young boy used other senses to see things that the living couldn't see. It didn't make the dead any more real just because this boy could see them. Energy of higher vibrations can pass through this apparent solidity that we call reality. Every object is 99.9999% space remember. Have you realized that your five senses are only experienced within your body? You can't for instance taste anything in the next room. Although you may think that you can hear or see something in the next room the sensation occurs in you. If it didn't you wouldn't be aware of it. The fact is that we can't experience anything that is hap-pening outside our beliefs. So what then is real if what we see is only a holographic illusion? May I suggest our experience of the illusion is real and the energy that comes into us through our chakras that makes the illusion for us.

Therefore if you want to change what your reality looks like you have to change the thought energy that is being beamed down from your Causal Body. While you can physically manipulate the illusion that is your reality you can't permanently change your experience of it unless you do this. Say for example you have a history of failures in a particular field of work. You can lie and cheat and manipulate your way throughout the company, even have people mis-credited for your failings but no amount of manipulation will stop your failings unless you change your energy.

Another example would be say a twisted back. You can have it manipulated every week but it will still go back to being twisted until you start looking at the cause of the twisting. It's like a plant that grows towards the light but you want it to grow in the opposite direction. You are going to have to remove the cause, i.e. the light or place the light in the opposite direction. No amount of pruning or training the plant will stop it growing towards the light.

In other words, using our analogy of the motion picture projector, you need to change the film that is running in the projector. Otherwise all the benefits of manipulation are short lived. It is your identity or Ego that wants to take the short cut to change your life to the way that it wants it to be. In doing so though it will be you who suffers. By letting the film run itself with the Etheric, Astral (Emotional) and Mental filters as clean as possible and with your chakras unblocked, you will ensure the sharpest focus and the least distorted reality. In those cases you will be a reflection of Light itself and not your Ego's idea of what it thinks is right. It will otherwise always lead to suffering. Always.

There are seven chakras in the physical body and five outside the physical body. The seven in the body have been thoroughly researched over the centuries and scientifically starting in the 20th century. However the body is more complicated than that and up to 72,000 Etheric points have been described as existing and interconnecting with the body's nervous and glandular system. More than that there are many sub-chakras. The major of these are in the hands, between the elbow and the wrist, the elbow and the shoulder, the hip and the knee, the knee and the ankle and the soles of the feet. Below that level of chakra there is another level of smaller chakras. And again and again many times until you have thousands of them.

Color is light vibrating at different frequencies. The chakras in the body correspond to the colors of the rainbow. Red, orange, yellow, green, blue, indigo, violet as they work themselves up our bodies from the tail-bone to the crown of the head. Because they are working on a vibrational level, the chakras reflect different emotional and mental moods within the person. Different energies correspond to different emotions and different emotions are linked to each of the colors. So as our emotions change, the intensity of that energy as seen in color does too. That means that each chakra is more or less activated depending on our moods or emotional blockages. The field surrounding our bodies is called our auric field. By seeing the auric field a person can tell what energy is predominating with that person at that time. It is an alternative form of diagnosis or insight into a person.

By identifying the blockage in the body by its physical symptoms, or by having the aura read by knowing what color corresponds to what strength, Fear, lesson in life to be learned, which Astral (Emotional) or Mental Body is affected, you could tell what you need to look at in order to heal yourself, and you can hasten your diagnosis and treatment.

It is through the chakras that chronic stress can negatively affect the body. The most critical imbalance is the one affecting the heart.

There are two different but equally detailed books on the chakras. One is written from the heart (feelings) and the other comes from the head (thoughts).

In *Anatomy of the Spirit: The Seven Stages of Healing* (published 1997 by Bantam Books) Caroline Myss explores, describes and explains the correlation between energy, body part and disease. She is insightful and talented as a healer and teacher and has put together a thorough, yet simply written, and very readable book. In her work she has assisted AIDS patients to be healed. The book is based on 15 years research and explores links between spiritual and emotional stresses and specific illnesses these create in different parts of the human energy system.

The other is *Vibrational Medicine: New Choices for Healing Ourselves* (by Dr. R Gerber published 1988 and subsequently revised by Bear & Co) and it is nothing short of brilliant for a scientific mind. Written from a empirical stand is it thoroughly convincing in proving the existence of chakras. Myss has spent 12 years researching alternative methods of diagnosis and healing.

After reading these books you can't but believe that chakras are real. In their own way they compliment one another. Heal these points of light entry and exit and you reality will start to shift—be brighter and clearer.

In the table below is a brief summary of each of the Chakras. It shows you which of the chakras relates to which element, the color of the chakra, the essence of the chakra and the theme. The Strengths column describes the positive attributes of the energy that the chakra exhibits and in Fears it tells you where your Fears are based. In other words if your Fear is abandonment then it is a first chakra disorder. The Physical Body column tells you where the relevant illness will occur in your physical body and how it affects your Emotional-Mental Body is described in that column. This Emotional-Mental body is an energy body that exists outside your Etheric Body and is described in full in the next chapter. Finally the last column gives examples of the types of diseases that affect you for the particular Fear or blockage that you may have in the chakra.

CHAKRA	STRENGTHS	FEARS	PHYSICAL BODY	EMOTIONAL – MENTAL BODY	ILLNESS
1. EARTH RED The material world, security – All is One	Tribal/family identity, bonding, tribal honor code, group safety, security, ability to provide for life's	Physical survival, abandonment by the group	COCCYGEAL, legs, bones, immune system, rectum, feet, spine, legs	The foundation of emotional mental health. These originate in the family.	Chronic lower back pain, sciatica, obsessive compulsive disorders,

	necessities, ability to stand up for self				mental illness out of family dysfunction, depression, varicose veins, rectal cancer, immune disorders
2. WATER ORANGE Sexuality, work, physical desire, pleasure – Honor One Another	To take risks, to recover from loss, to defend and protect ourselves, to rebel and build a life, ability and talent to make decisions	Losing control, e.g. through being a Victim	SACRAL, sex organs, pelvis, large intestine, lower back, appendix	Our need for relationships and to control our life, e.g. through money, positions of power	Lower back pain, impotence, problems with sex organs, pelvis, large intestine
3. FIRE YELLOW Ego, personality, Self Esteem, gathering feelings into light energy – Honor Oneself	Self respect, Self Esteem, self confidence, ambition, ethics, ability to handle a crisis and to take risks, generosity	Fear of rejection, criticism, humiliation, all Fears of how we look – esteem issues of weight, height, race	SOLAR PLEXUS Abdomen, stomach, gall bladder, upper intestine, liver, kidney, pancreas, adrenals, spleen	Personal power center, the core of our personality and Ego	AIDS, arthritis, hepatitis, gastric/duoden al ulcers, liver dysfunction, colon/intestina problems, indigestion, anorexia, bulimia
4. AIR GREEN	Love, compassion,	Loneliness, commitment,	HEART and all problems	Emotional perceptions are	Heart attack, asthma, lung

Love, forgiveness, abundance, compassion – Love is Divine power	forgiveness, hope, trust, inspiration, dedication	unable to protect ourselves emotionally, betrayal leading to jealousy, anger, hate, bitterness, unforgiveness	associated with it, lungs, shoulders, arms, ribs, breasts, thymus	housed here. As children our emotions weren't controlled but as adults they are.	cancer, pneumonia, allergies
5. BLUE will, self expression – Surrender Personal Will to Divine Will	Personal authority, faith, self knowledge, capacity to make decisions while being honest with yourself	The Will of a higher power.	THROAT, thyroid, trachea, neck, mouth, teeth, gums, esophagus, hypothalamus	Affects choice in our emotional and mental struggles. All illness is affected by choice	Sore throat, mouth ulcers, gum problems, swollen glands
6. INDIGO mind, intuition, insight, wisdom – Seek Only the Truth	Receiving inspiration, creativity, intuitive reasoning, understanding		THIRD EYE, brain, nervous system, ear, eyes, nose, pineal gland, pituitary gland	Links to our mental body, intelligence, psychological characteristics (a combination of facts, Fears, personal experiences, memories	Brain tumor, stroke, blindness, deafness, learning disabilities
7. VIOLET spirituality – Live in the Present Moment	Faith in a higher power, inner guidance, insight into healing, trust, devotion		HEAD, skin, muscles and bones	Inspiration, prophetic thoughts, transcendent ideas, mystical connections	Energetic disorders, chronic fatigue, extreme sensitivity to light and sound

4.31   Chakra One—Red

This is called the base chakra. It is the root that connects us to the Earth—the seat of our pants so to speak. It is the densest and most basic of the energies and as red signifies it is connected to passion, fire and Anger. Being the base chakra it relates to the energies of survival. And within survival the family and tribe come first. AIDS was a tribal issue in the gay community. It dealt with survival. The tribe was under attack and the disease manifested accordingly. It was also an issue of low Self Esteem and so affected the 3rd chakra as well. Related to the 1st chakra is honoring your family. It's where the will to live resides. Too much energy in this area could make you defensive. The energy can be directed creatively or towards a new life. The energy flows from this point up the spine through the higher chakras and in doing so aligns them.

4.32   Chakra Two—Orange

As the number two suggests, this chakra deals with partnership, marriage, diplomacy and relationships generally. It ties people together. Integrity and honor are the keys to a successful use of this energy. It also relates to joy, pleasure, happiness and abundance. Most men only operate from their first and second chakras. So between their house, job and a good time they don't really go much past that. But that is changing. They are now learning to open the higher chakras of intuition and Love.

4.33   Chakra Three—Yellow

You've all heard of gut instinct. The 3rd chakra is where your gut instinct is found. While the 2nd chakra is about a one-on-one relationship, the 3rd chakra is about larger relationships—clubs, groups, organizations, bands, associations, fellowships etc.—so it is also somewhat tribal in nature too. And it is about self respect. One works with the other. Without self respect our relationships can't have depth of intimacy. We can't be intimate because we don't like ourselves enough to share the deeper aspects of ourselves. We are ashamed of them. In some cases the associations become anonymous—for those with problems in this area the anonymity of the Internet is a boon. Because our Fear of being alone is so high (we don't have enough people around us) we can be possessive and jealous in trying to control and are afraid of being alone. Health comes from having a personal code of honor.

4.34   Chakra Four—Green

This is a pivotal point. The power of Love. Everything needs it to survive. When we are not loving we are out of balance and most strongly open to disease. If we don't forgive ourselves for what we think is wrong we are basically poisoning ourselves. A relationship teaches us to explore Love but we need to learn to Love ourselves first before we can Love another. A key message of this book is Love and it is explored in a very in-depth way in Chapter 7. In loving ourselves we must accept ourselves. This is a big challenge when you have advertising and Hollywood telling you that success belongs to the beautiful people and then showing you what beautiful is. In other words, success is rewarded with happiness and Love. It can be but not under these circumstances. That is the world of the Ego. True beauty shines out from a person and touches you, drawing you to them and uplifting you leaving you feeling peaceful and blissed out. So it doesn't matter how much plastic surgery you have, or what you wear. Often extreme forms of vanity are used to hide deep insecurities, low Self Esteem and self hatred. Unfortunately while these issues are masked by cosmetic surgery, the trappings of self importance, wealth, power and cosmetics themselves, these people will never be happy and will always be looking for more leading shallow lives, a facade to themselves and the world. Their dis-satisfaction with the unfulfilment that their looks and trappings bring eventually leads to diseases affecting their guts. If we do not nourish ourselves with Love (no amount of travel, food, sex, drugs or alcohol will compensate for that) then we become emotionally toxic and that toxicity bleeds into our relationships. An empty heart creates an empty life. By nature we are loving and thrive in harmony and tranquillity.

4.35   Chakra Five—Blue

This point connects the Heart (your Astral (Emotional) Body—see Chapter 5) with the Mind (your Mental Body—see Chapter 6). Now we move into more abstract areas of life. The energy here connects us to the Universe—of being open to guidance from a greater power—a divine power if you like. While the Ego runs your life you can't hear the whispers that your reality sends to you, nudging you to make decisions for your higher good and greater health and enjoyment of life. Put you Ego out of the way and you open yourself to divine guidance. With it thinking for you, miracles can occur in your life. A higher power has a better view of where you are and what energies are coming towards you than you can stuck down here in 3rd dimensional reality. It can steer you away from choices and people toward new opportunities, enjoyment and peace. It also means that the pain and struggle from making decisions and choices, which aren't the most beneficial for you, will stop. When you keep persevering sometimes your reality is saying to you—you are going the wrong way.

When you start questioning your purpose in life, start reading books like this one, and asking why, why why, then you'll know you are ready for help and to change. You'll start to see your limitations and how unfulfilling material success really is when you are using it as a substitute for having a relationship with yourself. Often you will reach this point because of a crisis in your life—illness, death, loosing a job, divorce—or all of them at once if it is major wake up call, which proves how incapable we are of doing it all by ourselves. Sometimes you just have to sit down and throw your arms up in the air and say— I give up. Only then will the help come to you.

The essence of this energy is to have Faith. Eventually you realize that personal power is limited. You can't control. No amount of success or standing can ever satisfy you. We are limited as people. Only the Universe is unlimited. The crisis you suffer could be enough to bring you to your knees- and if it does not, life will get very tough and stagnation will follow then death. The Fear is not going forward with this energy is that you will lose your material success and identity. But you don't and you don't have to. You were always intended to have it all. To be a success was part of the divine plan. You don't see the plants and animals falling over themselves to fail do you? Why should you be making it hard for yourself just because you can think and can make choices? Spirituality is all about expansion of energy. Fear is all about limitation, not sharing, denial. When you were a child what did your religion teach you about how spirituality should be? Another name for spirituality is Love. What sort of life do you have—one of limitation, mediocrity and struggle or expansion and happiness?

4.36   Chakra Six—Indigo

This chakra unites your Mind (your Mental Body—see Chapter 6) with your psyche (the conscious and Unconscious psychological force that is your Causal Body—see Chapter 7). This leads to intuitive insight or what is called wisdom. When you get that, then personal growth and self awareness really starts getting into top gear, as your Mind opens, you take back your power from the false Ego truths (drugs, addictions, non growth behaviors), discriminating between thoughts motivated by strength or Fear—in other words growing up into an adult and no longer creating your reality from Ego, denial and your childhood and adolescent beliefs that don't serve you. This is the path to true and long lasting health and an enjoyable life where you get to have everything you want.

Life is all about accommodating change. You can't hang onto anything. Resisting change makes it worse. The more you resist something the more energy you put into creating it—so that eventually you create the thing you don't want and not the thing that you do want. In other words you are creating using the energy of Fear, limitation, pain and struggle and not the energy of Love, joy, happiness and peace. To do this you need to learn the lesson of detachment. To let go. Not to hang on to anything or anyone. To give up control and manipulation. You can no longer hang onto the past, your partner, career, an expected result, wanting, material possession—you could loose them all in a moment's time. If you were not detached that would take you to crisis. You've seen the Victims of natural disasters absolutely distraught. They've lost everything. They were tied to their material possessions. By creating at this higher level of energy instead of through your Ego these disasters are not problems or set-backs. They are true opportunities for you to create more. If you created something once—then you can create it again. You already know how to do it. If you blame outside circumstances for the crisis that is buying into the holographic illusion that you created and treating it as real. This will blind you to the bigger picture and keep you stuck in unhappiness.

4.37   Chakra Seven—Violet

Most people are either living in the past (blame, shame, Guilt based realities) or the future (anxiety, stress, Fear based realities). Once you start mastering the energy of this chakra then you have arrived in reality as it really is. The past is gone. The future is an illusion. You realize that there is really is only the now in which you can live. You are now ready to work with the energy of spiritual mastery.

When aligned with the energy of this chakra you become another person—it is as though you have shed a skin and moved beyond the ordinary realms of existence. Everything is different. There develops a devotion to something greater than yourself. The spiritual crisis that you encounter can be what is called "the dark night of the Soul". When you reach this point in your life many of you will have undergone your crisis. Now you are entering the energy of devotion.

4.38   The Remaining Chakras

Very little research has been done on the remaining 5 chakras owing to their recent discovery. These energy chords connect you directly into the Universe. The point from which your energy originally comes.

The 8th is positioned between the feet and looks like you are standing on a water fountain. It is the chakra of transformation and elimination and is colored brown. Here you will find the energy of new beginnings.

The 9th resonates to the color pink while the 10th resonates to Pearl. These streams of energy connect us deep into space to a larger source of energy from which we are all related.

The 11th is silver and represents the power of the male energy of doing or what we call God. The 12th is gold and represents the power of the female energy of being and is the energy of the Goddess.

Chapter 5

—THE ASTRAL (OR EMOTIONAL) BODY

Beyond the Etheric Body is what's called the Astral Body but I'll refer to it as the Emotional Body because then it's easier to remember what it is all about. It's of a higher frequency than the Etheric Body. Unlike the Etheric Body, which oversees cellular, hormonal and glandular function, this field is involved with experiencing, expressing and repressing emotion. If this emotional energy is distorted or discordant then that imbalance will flow into the body through the energy meridians that connect the energy fields to the physical body (the chakras—see previous Chapter 4.3) into the glands and this eventually will cause illness.

Emotion is a combination of the words "E" being the scientific abbreviation of Energy (as in $E=mc^2$) and "motion" meaning "moving". Therefore e-motion is energy in motion. Energy that you create in your body which moves through your body. It is what you feel. You feel the energy. You can't rationalize it. It is the opposite to thinking. You can't think and feel at the same time. You can't feel 2 emotions simultaneously. You can fluctuate between them. Sometimes the emotion is so strong you can't think at all, e.g. mad with rage and you are said to be irrational.

The Emotional Body is impacted by the emotional experiences from our life—past relationships, profound or traumatic memories and it relates to experiencing, expressing and repressing emotion. Science has proven that neuropeptides—the chemicals triggered by emotions—are thoughts that have converted into matter. These emotional experiences become encoded in our bodies by being physically stored in our cell membranes—or memory-brains. And this is the important point here. What it means is that your Mind and your body are part of the same entity. Your memory of the experience is not in your brain—it is in your body because the same kinds of cells that manufacture and receive emotional chemistry in the brain are present in the body. The brain is a receptor, a forward thinking device and a transmitter. It is a processor. Your body is the storage component of the processed data.

The membranes then generate an energy that describes what is in the membrane, e.g. the emotion of Self Pity or of a happy go lucky attitude. A psychic can read these in your energy field. That is what psychics do. They have the intuitive ability to receive by image or sound or sensation that your energy field is sending out. Some psychics use a medium to help them read or interrupt this information, e.g. tarot cards, tea leaves or even stones—anything that will focus their attention. To the trained observer or psychic s/he can tell the emotional state that the person is in. This is relevant particularly in cases of psychic counseling and healing which is discussed in Chapter 13.6.

Where you have had a negative experience, e.g. humiliation, whenever the circumstance arises again that created the experience, your body would react in a similar way. Also with positive experiences, e.g. being rewarded or acknowledged by your peers for a success. This makes you feel powerful every time you think about it. So the more success you have and the more you focus on it the more success you will have. Some people received a "knock" in childhood that they have never recovered from and the information stored in their cells is still transmitting the same message, e.g. "I am a Victim. I am powerless. I have no control of what happens to me I my life". All of this is true for that person because it is their experience but it isn't necessarily true for the person sitting next to them. Their resentment of those for whom it is not true will eventually in some way contribute to them becoming diseased later in life. Interestingly where you would have a whole community thinking that it is not as good as another could lead to that community en mass developing a disease that reflects that belief.

Your emotional energy impacts on your physical body and becomes your body. What your body becomes is as a result of what you experience. Your experiences come from your beliefs. Your beliefs are the empowerment of your thoughts. You have all seen the hunched over old people who carry their experiences of life on their backs—crippling them. Or the timid person afraid of everything, exhibiting nervous tendencies. Most of us conceal the impact that our experiences have had on us. Most people deny the negative ones and when their bodies become too full of the denied energy, they stop functioning because they are out of balance. The body becomes diseased. The popular diseases this century are cancer and heart. Last century it was something else. Have you noticed that just as the human race gets rid of one disease another unheard of disease surfaces to replace it! It is an on going process arising from the polarity. Some diseases come back in a different form because the previous disease was never healed. Only the symptoms were cured. So you may think that you have healed the body but if you haven't healed the memory in the cells have you healed anything other than the symptoms of the disease? Sometimes a disease is healed. A "cure" is the physical manifestation that a disease has been healed on an energetic level, e.g. new beliefs have been formed or emotional blockages released. The energetic healing comes first because the body is a projection of the higher forms of energy that are creating it. The body merely manifests the resonance of the energy fields.

Your physical body is bio-feedback system. It is an instrument that you can learn to read by understanding what the messages of the imbalance are trying to tell you. That is where true healing starts. If you stifle the symptoms then there are no clues from which to read the messages. A lot of Western medicine is more concerned with treating symptoms than finding the energetic causes of disease. Bacteria and viruses are only the physical manifestations exhibiting biologically to make the disease present. This explains why one person will get a disease but the person standing next to them will not. An infectious disease is only infectious because the people catching the disease all have similar resonance in their energy fields and belief systems. Why didn't the HIV epidemic spread into the community at large in America, Europe, Australia and the developed parts of Asia. The potential was there. And why is it limited to manifesting only amongst people who are powerless, have low Self Esteem and see themselves as belong to a particular class of person? The reason is that the rest of the population believed something else.

Emotions are a warning to you that you have moved out of the NOW. Where emotions are present it is a clue to you that your thoughts have moved either into the future (with its anxiety, Fear and stress) or into the past (where blame, Guilt and shame live). The Mind exists in the next higher energy field beyond the emotional body. The thoughts from here pass down through the emotional body into the Etheric Body and manifest in your physical body. Whenever you are in your emotions you will know that you are telling yourself a story because you will be experiencing the results of it, i.e. that your beliefs are manifesting as your reality. These stories that you tell yourself keep you from being in the now or the present moment. They may be true for you but they are preventing you from seeing what is really going on in your life. The story is only the clue to you seeing beyond it to how your beliefs are creating your reality. Division III will tell you how to use the energy of the emotional body to bring your emotional energy back into alignment.

5.1   FEAR

While Love itself is a state of being that has no opposite—it is above polarity, Fear is an emotion which can be said to be the opposite of Love because it creates a reality the opposite to what Love does.

Fear is distorted female energy. It is a denial of Love. This emotion reinforces powerlessness and hinders positive progress in life. It is a contracting energy not an expanding energy like Love. In weather terms—Fear is a low pressure system drawing all energy down into it as it spirals down. While Love is the accelerator energy of your reality, Fear is the brake in that reality creation.

Fear is physical in nature—fright unanswered turns to Fear and Fear is also emotional in nature—you can experience Fear without any facts to support you or justify you feeling it. For no reason at all you just feel afraid. Be aware though that the emotional Fears are only influences in your reality. They are not controls. You have believed that your outside world is real (and not the projection of beliefs that it really is) and thinking it was real you gave it your power, i.e. you act in response to what is happening in the world because you think that it is controlling what you can and can't do. You have been unaware that you are creating that world in the first place. What happens is that you believe that Fear (an event outside you) causes your reality to be as it is. You believe that the Fear is real. Then, having created a reality of Fear you respond to that reality with more Fear. You are in fact just frightening yourself. Have you noticed how more and more Fear is present in the media. Most people live in a Fear based reality. Fear is the basis of all disease. So how can you get well if you are motivated by Fear? Fear is the food of Ego. It thrives on it to keep you under its control. So you are using your internal Fears as the source of your external reality.

5.11   The Source of All Fear

If you can understand where Fear came from it will help you to be less afraid of it. You will know what you are dealing with.

The original state of being was Love. This was the source of creation itself. When we as consciousness separated from that Love (in biblical terms, forced from the Garden of Eden) Fear was experienced. The Garden of Eden was where no one worked but no one was hungry and everyone had a house and no one ever got ill. This was a dimension of no polarity. Of only Love. Heaven on Earth. The female energy became distorted after being polarized and likewise with the male energy after it also became polarized. This polarization occurred when Adam and Eve began to think, became aware of themselves as a result of their Egoic personality and were able to choose between polarities which they were now able to see as a result of being able to differentiate. The story of Adam and Eve isn't limited to Christianity and can be found the world over in other cultures.

The original emotion became Fear and the original Fear became loosing the Love of the Universe (i.e. God)—our nourishment—or to put it another way Fear of loosing our connection with Love. That Fear became Fear of loneliness—the result that came from loosing our connection with Love. From that Fear all Fears came. All Fears can be traced back to Fear of loneliness. As the polarities increased other emotions developed.

Fear of loneliness is a symptom of the fact—
1.   You do not trust yourself to deal with reality alone.
2.   You do not think that you Love good enough.
3.   You are feeling separate from the Universe.

Fear is a symptom of beliefs that don't work, that is, faulty beliefs. Beliefs create reality remember. The belief "I don't Love good enough" was the original faulty belief from which Fear of separation from Love came and therefore it was the faulty belief from which all Fears come. So the experience of not loving good enough was to not have Love.

When there is too little male energy or too little female energy then Fear comes up.

Fear of separation became a means to bring your consciousness back to Love and so it became the impetus for the great spiritual journey for the Soul i.e. to go back to Love and in doing so to learn who you really are. You are on that journey now. Reading this book is proof of that. In finding out who you are you will come to see more and more that the end of that journey is in front of you now. You just haven't seen that yet. What you have been looking for has been in front of you all the time. More than that, the answers have been inside you all along. You've been looking outside for the answers. You've been looking in the wrong place.

The purpose of Fear is to slow you down. Love will accelerate you. So it was intended that Fear would slow you down and you could then return to Love. But the Fear of loneliness was denied—and as the result of denial is to amplify that which is being denied—the loneliness got greater, so Love seemed to be further away and the separation from Love therefore became greater. So the Fear increased and the spiral got bigger and the Fear increased.

Fear then became a motivator in your reality creation process and you used it as your reference for doing or not doing something. So Fear became an accelerator instead of a brake. Have you ever seen what happens to a car when you have your foot on the brake and the accelerator at the same time? You sped off out of control. You weren't able to use Love to create your reality. But in the Fear you got scared and forgot how to get back to Love. Everything then can be traced back to Fear. Everything in our lives became a means of getting back to Love. This is the bottom line. This is the motivation behind everything that we do.

So the potential Fear of loneliness became loneliness and everything else became a means to overcome that loneliness—all the blame, the righteousness, the Self Pity, the Negative Ego, the hype, the lies, the pretense, the manipulation, the Martyr and the self importance. Anyone not in a state of Love therefore is ultimately coming from a place of loneliness and acting to assuage that loneliness. Everyone is therefore coming from a place of Fear. So you can see that ultimately everyone on the planet is seeking only one thing—Love. If you know this, then the world starts to make a lot of sense. And compassion (which is a form of Love) becomes easier to dispense.

The many forces of the world then used this Fear of loneliness for their own purposes—

1. **The Christian belief in Mythology**: Adam & Eve were faced with an angry God. Their Fear—original sin for which we will never be forgiven. The taught faulty belief is "if I'm good, I struggle and endure pain then I'll be forgiven, perhaps". Unfortunately the same beliefs teach that you won't know till judgment day and so you are driven out of Fear of loneliness to lead a hard life atoning for sin, working hard to prove your worth. The fact is you are by divine right worthy of Love. In essence you are Love on an energetic level seeking Love. You stop you from receiving Love because of a story you choose to believe. Humanity has been in denial for thousands of years. It is in the interests of those who need to control out of Fear, who keep everyone else in a state of Fear. Fear sells newspapers and cinema tickets. It keeps the Fearful in church, living in hope that in spite of their sinfulness that God will forgive them. We Love Fear. It's an old friend, comfortable and warm inside us—in a perverse way—and we can play with it to frighten people and thereby get a cheap hit of power.

2. **Parents**. Fear of abandonment comes from Fear of loneliness. Your first day at school could have felt like abandonment leaving mother or father behind. Home sickness is a Fear of abandonment. Childhood circumstances of Fear all come from Fear of abandonment. Parents use this Fear to control. Fear of adoption has been known to be used to scare a child to behave. The potential pain and Fear of loneliness that was experienced as children was worse than the pain you put yourself through as children in order to get a parent's attention. The threat of being abandoned was more devastating than being abandoned.

3. **Maturation Process**. In adolescence (a period of extremes when you would just die of humiliation if your mother/father ever turned up to take you home from your peer group meeting) it was a Fear of rejection. "You won't be part of the group". You'll be 'alone' is the Fear. In adulthood it is also Fear of rejection. "No one will Love me" is the faulty belief "so I have to

belong" is the solution and you acquiesce out of Fear. In old age it becomes Fear of loneliness again. "I'm not needed any more" is the faulty belief. Again it becomes Fear of abandonment. As Fear is an energy that you think then if you put enough energy into it (denied or conscious) you will end up manifesting the thought and you end up lonely. Look at so many old people. Alone and afraid.

The pain in loosing someone to death is the pain of separation from Love. In those cases we have projected our self worth onto the deceased who gave us Love. We have been attached to them. With them gone we feel the void. To overcome this you need to learn to generate the Love from within first. Then you have an endless source of Love that no one can ever take away from you. Death reminds us on a Soul level of the separation that we feel as consciousness from the Universe which is a state of Love—a state that we forewent in order to incarnate on this Planet.

Personal growth is you using your free will to separate from the harmony of the Universe—Love. To learn to grow is to stretch then to self motivate yourself and return to Love from that stretch or separation. This is what you are doing now. This is the journey that everyone on the Planet is on—whether they know it or not.

5.12   What Then Is Fear?

1. **Fear is a thing**. It's not just your imagination. Every time you think of it you are adding to it. Dwell on it and it gets bigger. In your reality you have spent more time thinking of Fear than Love so Fear is bigger on Earth.

2. **You invite Fear in**. You can also send it away. It is potent. You add your power to it and it becomes dangerous. It will leave when asked. It really will. Fear can be commanded to leave.

3. Fear **can't be destroyed**. Energy can only be transmuted or transcended or transformed.

4. Fear is **dumb**—like all emotions when used negatively.

5. Fear is **repetitive**—your Fears today are the same as yesterday, e.g. "I won't get the job" is the same Fear as "I won't get on the team".

From Fear comes blockages and limitations. From blockages and limitations negativity thrives. So all negativity comes from Fear and ultimately it comes from Fear of loneliness.

5.13   The Positive Qualities of Fear

Fear can be both positive and negative. So Fear is a real emotion. A real emotion is any emotion that can be expressed positively or negatively. For example, Anger expressed honestly creates change. It is the Anger repressed within you that kills you. If you act out of that repressed Anger then you are not clear about what you are doing and are doing it for some reason other than one of Love. You usually are striking out or hurting others.

1. Fear can be **a warning** to pay attention to your reality. It is saying "there's something to be aware of".Fear is like a smoke alarm. It produces anxiety but less than the anxiety of the burning flesh you will experience if you have removed the batteries from the smoke alarm because you didn't like the sound of it.

2. Fear can let you know **where you lack trust**. Where are you afraid? It's saying "I don't trust in those areas". What aren't I trusting myself to handle? e.g. the phone calls or letters I will not take or open. This is from Fear of the unknown. What won't you handle?

3. Fear can be **the brakes to slow you down**. Fear creates friction to slow down the inertia or momentum that the "push me-pull me" action of Love produces. Fear initially was meant to slow you down in your separation from Love and to be your gravitational return to Love but you denied your Fear and kept going, increasing your Fear, denying it more and more until

eventually it will destroy you. ALL illness ultimately comes from Fear.

4.   Fear will tell you where **you have a faulty belief**. Where your beliefs are not working for you. Fear is a big aid to letting you know who you are.

5.14   The Negative Qualities of Fear

What is wrong with Fear? In order to conquer Fear you have to know what it is and why it is and why you can't allow it to continue to enslave you.

1.   Fear **separates you from you**, your identity, your thoughts, feelings and your reality and any sense that you create your own reality. That's why some people get angry and violent when the concept of you create your own reality is put to them. How afraid must they be? It makes you blame everyone out there for what is happening to you.

2.   Fear **paralyses**—prevents you from change. It holds you in a place of boredom, projection, identification, inertia, jealousy, revenge, doubt (in the form of Anger, Guilt and depression) and Self Pity. A little Fear numbs you. Unrequited it grows and engulfs and paralyzes you making you unable to be intimate, to act, think, feel, to be responsible, to laugh, give or to be able to ask for help (a cause of AIDS). So it should not be hard to pick anyone in Fear. Most people live in a Fear based reality.

3.   Fear **perpetrates the past** and the Ego, which feeds upon it. You are afraid of the unknown and use the past to repeat itself because it is familiar. You re-hash old thoughts and beliefs to create your reality afraid of what you might create otherwise. Your Ego feeds on Fear and keeps you there.

4.   Fear is **addictive**. The longer you go without something going wrong in your life the greater you know how bad its going to be when it goes wrong. Fear of the future (anxiety) grows bigger the more things go right in your world. You get angry at

anyone who tries to take away your Fear. You can't believe that a day can go by without Fear. It's your belief and belief creates reality. So you have to keep Fear around to hit you over the head with it so you know you are alive.

5.   Fear is **accommodating**—it lets you keep all your rationalizations, game plays, manipulations and dominating tactics. "But I'm scarred" is your excuse for doing it. Just admitting your Fear doesn't justify manipulation. It sounds like you are being responsible by admitting the Fear but it isn't really being responsible You are using Fear as an excuse to hurt others and to behave badly.

6.   Fear **fuels your emotional blockages**. By definition your blockages came from Fear in the first place. Your blockages are your faulty beliefs that are producing realities that you do not want. So when you meet your hurdles in your life you become more fearful of them. And this becomes a repeating pattern. Fear keeps you stuck.

7.   Fear **separates you from Love**—the thing that you want more than anything else—the only thing that can complete you and make you feel real. You crave it—whether you are aware of it or not. The lack of it is the greatest suffering that there can be. With no Love in your life this leads to a denial of the Universe (a greater power than you are) and this is a denial of Love itself. The more you deny Love the more Fear you experience in your life. The more Fear you experience the more Fear you will experience. It is a vicious circle that leads to resentment, bitterness and selfishness. By the time you get old you are terrified and lock yourself away from the world. Look at the life of the elderly generally. Ridden with disease and afraid of change, locked in their homes afraid to go out. Those who play on Fear are exposing the extent to which they have been cut off from Love. Their manipulation is a scream of "I'm lost".

5.15   Why Do We Have Fear?

In its negative sense a pay off is a benefit that you aren't consciously aware of but it is something you want. It's like receiving payola behind your back. You know you are getting it but you deny it. It's not as much as you would like but it's better than nothing. It's a sell out of your integrity. The pay off is too sweet for you to give up the painful and often destructive and limiting way that you get it even though by giving up those means you could get more of what you want. In almost every case it stops you receiving Love.

LIFE WITH FEAR	LIFE WITHOUT FEAR (which is life with Love)
The payoffs -	The pay offs -
(a) You get to avoid all responsibility, choice, change, adulthood.	(a) You accept freedom, creativity and to creatively control your reality.
(b) You get to blame almost anyone you want to and Love those who say Fear is real. If Fear weren't real you'd loose your excuse to rely on it.	(b) You accept yourself. Build confidence and ambition.
(c) You get to be righteous—being afraid justifies everything.	(c) You get to feel real, totally honest with your Fears and Loves.
(d) Fear guarantees the survival of the Ego. It feeds on Fear. Loves it. And because you gave your power to your Ego you need to keep it in that place for your survival – to continue your identity.	(d) There is no guarantee and you are therefore free to create, do and be what you want.
(e) Fear is a source of Self Pity.	(e) Self Love, Self Esteem.
(f) Fear is a reason to make you struggle. To struggle is noble and gives you a sense of self importance and that makes you	(f) Self confidence and self worth.

	struggle. To struggle is noble and gives you a sense of self importance and that makes you feel important and better than those who do not struggle. It is false esteem.		
(g)	You get to rationalize and justify your manipulations. Its what makes it OK to hurt, lie and to destroy. Your excuse is "I was scared" and you think that justifies everything. You are really saying "I admitted my Fear now you do something about it". You are hiding in Fear. One day you won't come out and you'll be buried alive suffocating.	(g)	Freedom. No past to hinder you.

If you look at what a life is like without Fear then you see what a life would be like with Love.

5.16   Why Haven't You Conquered Fear Previously?

1. **The pay offs** are the blockages, the avoidance, the blame and the self righteousness. Part of you wants to feel the Self Pity, the self importance, wants to cling to the past and wants a justification or guarantee before proceeding. Even though its damming, damaging and self punishing the pay offs keeps you stuck.

2. **You are enslaved** to it—through paralysis, addiction and accommodation. And you keep fearing because you are afraid not to. You don't want to believe its possible. You get angry and critical of those who don't live in Fear.

3. You are enjoying a **false sense of power** by manipulating others.

4.   You've been cut off from Love but **don't believe or know that you create your own reality** and that the Universe exists so you say "I'm the Universe. I'm all that is". You are really saying "help". You are lost in Fear and exposing the damage Fear has done. You've not forgiven yourself for not conquering Fear yet. If you don't admit 1 and 2 and 3 above then you won't forgive yourself and then you won't be able to conquer Fear.

When you conquer Fear you'll know there is a greater power and Love that is available to you. It will be real to you. Forgive yourself first then you can conquer Fear.

5.   Society reinforces Fear as a **positive motivator** especially in films and computer games. You feel alive and charged with adrenaline when you see Fear. Violence on TV and in computer games is an outlet for playing out that Fear. Problem is some people don't know where reality stops and starts if they spend too much time in these so-called recreational activities. If violent computer games were so recreational the Army wouldn't be using them to train their soldiers to kill.

Even children's G rated cartoon are rife with violence teaching children at an early age that violence is OK. In a study published in the 24 May 2000 edition of the Journal of the American Medical Association two researchers examined 74 G-rated theatrical films available on video and found that each contained at least one act of violence. At least one character was injured in 46 of the movies and at least one was killed in half of the films. The movies averaged 9.5 minutes of violence, with the 1998 King Arthur tale "Quest for Camelot" containing violence in almost 30% of the movie. The researchers said they believe their study included every G-rated theatrical feature available on video before September 1999

If you want to know more about the proven relationship between violent behavior and violent computer games go to www.time.com/personal or email Amy Dickinson at timefamily@aol.com. The facts now speak for themselves. People use Fear to escape from their other day to day problems. They need something that strong to overcome their reality. Eventually how much global Fear do they need to create—a war maybe, a gas shortage, air pollution?—something life threatening. The downside is that Fear will kill you. You are playing with fire when you play with Fear.

The successful person acts in spite of Fear. You tend to get jealous of them. They still have Fear but they won't let it control them. Everything is just a matter of choice. Fear stands in your way. This is why success is not as encouraging as it could be. Love is success.

Being Fearful you become defensive assuming a position of helplessness or becoming aggressive, wanting to control. Fear is a mask to hide behind. If you are Fearful in a relationship you will either seek control of the relationship or else allow yourself to be dominated. By choosing Fear as a response to a situation you affirm that you are susceptible to becoming a Victim or giving up your power (this is powerlessness).

Fear instigates Anger, which in turn causes separation and pain. Fear is behind self punishment, which is a cause of illness. So is Anger.

Fear is also recognized by judgment (where one is critical and rejects), pity (a belief that the object of the pity is a Victim of circumstance), resentment (a defensive attitude indicating an Unconscious desire to attack), superficiality (pretentious behavior), self punishment (from rejecting yourself) and insensitivity (towards the feelings of others).

You wouldn't think of these as being aspects of Fear but they are. How many of you know people (including yourselves) who demonstrate these qualities? Once you can see that they are really only examples of Fear then it is easier to understand what you are dealing with. Treat it as Fear not as what you see it to be. That is the most efficient way to deal with it.

5.2   ANGER

What I will talk about in this section of the book is suppressed or repressed Anger—the Anger that is denied. Anger of itself is neither good nor bad. It is only an emotion. It's what we do with the Anger that matters. Expressed inappropriately then it becomes negative. Expressed appropriately it can be positive, e.g. as a motivator for you to give up an addictive behavior. Suppressed or repressed Anger is dangerous to you, your life and everything and everyone in it.

5.21   How Does Anger Hurt And Destroy?

If Anger is denied it will be processed in your life anyway. It is an emotion—an energy—that continues to move. There are a number of ways that Anger will come out.

1. **Physically in your body** either in the physical body itself as disease, e.g. cancer or in the Mental Body through the Negative Ego. Every major physical health problem that you have is associated with denied Anger. As for your Ego, it feeds on Anger. According to a study published in the British medical journal Lancet, of 13,000 people it was shown that people who are Anger prone have three times the risk of heart attack. Later in Chapter 6.1 I will talk about the Ego in full detail. At the moment believe me when I say that it is a power grabbing device which gets its power by interpreting what happens in your reality. It uses Anger as a filter and tinges your view of the world through it. You have given your Ego the responsibility of giving you the reasons as to what is happening in your world as well as the responsibility for giving you the facts. In this way you let it rationalize your world. The Ego puts ideas into your head and you believe them. These ideas are distorted with Anger.

2. **In your external world**—Anger will be fueled, e.g. you won't get that promotion, you are stuck with the people you don't

like but have to work with every day, you 're bored, you can never seem to pay all your bills, there are always unforeseen expenses that come up just as you get ahead and fights with strangers. This is Anger bleeding out into your reality.

3. **In your relationships**—a relationship is a reflection of you at an intimate level. If you have denied Anger then that is where it will come out. Most often this happens with parents and Lovers. The purpose of a relationship is for you to have a mirror in which to see yourself. What you see and for how long you choose to stand there and see it is up to you. The only real way to deal with what you see is to own it, to accept it and to take responsibility for it. Changing the image is only a temporary solution as it will come back in another form at another time. Real change comes from within.

4. **Your Self Esteem is damaged**—true Self Esteem comes from within through honesty, integrity, responsibility and trust. If Anger is denied you can't live honestly because you aren't expressing or admitting to all of who you are. You are lying to yourself. Integrity is living spontaneously. You can't be spontaneous if you have denied Anger. It stops you from acting. You create your own reality means you take responsibility for your life. The more you take responsibility the more powerful you become. But if you are expressing Anger covertly out into your reality through your Ego, you are not going to want to nor be able to take responsibility for anything that your Anger might be doing. You can't. You've denied that it is your Anger and therefore you are denying that it is you who are doing it. So you intellectualize and further deny responsibility for anything that is happening in your reality and this in turn creates more Anger that you deny further and the vicious circle continues. You then develop the emotional blockage of Victimhood and become a Victim of your reality—it's a perverse form of reality creation. A full explanation of Victimhood is to be found later in this chapter at Chapter 5.42. To trust yourself you must be able to go into

your Sub-conscious and get the information that you need on which to base your decisions and actions. I talk about the Sub-conscious in more detail in Chapter 6.21. It is part of the higher vibration of your consciousness. If you are clouded with Anger then you can't trust yourself because you never know what you are going to create next. You've given your reality creative ability to your Ego. If you can't trust yourself then you can't trust your reality either. You never know what is going to happen next. This is stressful amongst other things—always waiting for the other shoe to fall.

So with no connection to the four pillars of your Self Esteem you have to look to your outside reality for validation. The Ego is exceptionally active here. When that happens you feel unfulfilled and always looking for more. You become highly competitive, powerless and resentful. Therefore it produces more Anger. Denied Anger produces Anger. The whole issue of denial is dealt with at Chapter 6.3 in the section on the Shadow.

5.   **Self Love & Self Forgiveness** suffer. You express Anger either inwardly or outwardly. If you are angry (whether or not you know it) it is difficult to Love and to forgive. Self forgiveness becomes self blame, self punishment and self ridicule and this is being self destructive. This is not to be confused with laughing at yourself. You are after all the silliest thing in your reality.

6.   People use **Guilt** to suppress Anger. There's a big section on Guilt later in this chapter at 5.4. Guilt is Anger that you feel that you do not have a right to have. If you have Guilt you feel that you do not have the right to feel happy and to be successful. Forget Guilt. It serves no purpose at all.

7.   **Depression** is Anger that you feel that you will get into trouble for having. So you put away all those tiny insignificant incidents that were too small to even think about again until one day you wake up paralyzed and weighed down with depression. Too depressed to move. Everything has become such a huge effort. For depression to be classified as a mental illness usually you

have to feel depressed for two weeks but anyone who has ever felt depressed knows that they do not have to feel depressed for 2 weeks to know that they are depressed. Depression is felt as either a persistent feeling of sadness or emptiness and/or a loss of interest or pleasure in activities or hobbies that were once enjoyed including sex. Of the following additional eight symptoms at least five have to be experienced as well before a clinical diagnosis of depression is made. These are—

a)   feelings of helplessness, worthlessness and Guilt,

b)   insomnia, early morning awakening or over sleeping,

c)   a change in appetite,

d)   decreased energy, fatigue and feeling 'slowed down',

e)   restlessness and irritability,

f)   difficulty concentrating and remembering,

g)   thoughts of suicide or suicide attempts and

h)   persistent physical symptoms that do not respond to medical treatment.

Unless you have looked at your Anger and released it then if any of these things are happening to you then you have denied Anger. In a study of 8,000 people published in the Archives of Internal Medicine it was found that depression increases the risk of heart attack by 72%. Depression appeared to double the risk for men. Ever heard the phrase "he died of a broken heart?" Great sadness will kill you.

5.22   Why Do We Suppress & Deny Anger?

1.   We were **taught as children** to do so—what I call the 'usual suspects'—firstly by mother, then father, school teachers, society, government and religion. "Don't be angry and don't express it if you are".

2.   It is **part of the male/female identity polarity**. It comes with the territory of being male or female in other words. Being male has always meant being always in control, not showing your emotions, not feeling, being sensitive and even tempered.

Being female has always meant being sweet, kind and demure. If a woman wasn't she was considered to be a bitch or pushy and these types of people made everyone feel uncomfortable. In the movie *Erin Brockovich*, Julia Roberts is a pushy bitch and we all love her for fighting for the noble cause. This is an indication as to how far we have come in breaking down that stereotype. Scarlett O'Hara was another role model who helped break down that stereotype. All the same the underlying belief is that you will be punished if you express your Anger. When Erin gets angry in the witness box she looses her case and Scarlett looses her men.

3. As an adult it is **part of your spiritual teaching**. Eastern philosophy says that you should rise above Anger. Western says that you should be calm and give Love in the face of it. That isn't easy to do because if you have Anger in your vibration then everything that goes out from you passes through that Anger veil and then has to pass through the Anger veil for the person that you are dealing with. By the time they get it then it is not what you sent out to them. It will come back to them as sweet Anger.

    Spiritual people handle their Anger cleanly. They acknowledge that they have it and deal with it appropriately, not dumping it on other people. This is the true meaning of detachment—it doesn't affect you. Indifference on the other hand means something else and this is what the quasi –spiritual person does.

4. **They do not know how to deal with it appropriately**.

5. **Anger makes people feel alive**. They use it as a motivation.

6. **It sustains the Ego**. The Ego is all concerned about being "better than" what it compares itself to or "worse than". So if it can't be better than then it becomes worse than and prides itself on that. The Ego thus uses Anger to motivate.

7. **Anger gives a false sense of power**. People think that power is the ability to have power over, i.e. control, influence, domination. They keep their Anger in place as a threat in order to

control, e.g. "if you don't do what I say then I will get angry". Angry people are often called powerful when the truth is that they are not powerful but just angry.

8.   **You Like It**. It's fun to be angry. It feels good. Letting off steam you call it. It can also be nostalgic—a reminder of how it felt to be a child.

5.23   The Pay Offs of Holding Onto Anger

In order to release your denied Anger you need to understand what your pay offs are—the so called unseen benefits that come "under the table" that are more worthwhile to your Ego's blockages and vested interests in your negativity than they are to your growth as a person. What are the benefits that you think are too good to give up?

1.   You get **to avoid taking responsibility** for your actions. You can use Anger as an excuse for punishing yourself and others. In other words you do not have to behave. Your excuse is that you were angry. Therefore you do not have to take responsibility for the impact you have on other people and you can deny that you make them angry.

2.   You get **to punish** e.g. your parents, school teachers, bosses and lovers. You can claim "they made me this way". It's an excuse you are choosing to believe. You are responsible for your own emotions. You choose to have them. They are yours and no one else's. It's another case of avoiding responsibility. In fact you can't wait to tell us your stories of mis-treatment. You regale in them. They are part of your identity. The Ego just Loves this stuff and feeds the illusion constantly.

3.   You get **to be righteously angry**. This is such a good pay off and we've all seen it in action. What happens is that you store up all your little Angers and keep them in an arsenal. Then one day someone comes along and happens to injure you in some way—it's the straw that breaks the camels back, e.g. bumps into you, cuts in line, a waiter spills soup on you or

takes too long to serve you. All hell breaks lose and you dump that arsenal of Anger righteously but out of proportion to the indignity. Then having inappropriately let it go you get to feel good about yourself and go back to stock piling more for the next Victim.

4. You get **a guarantee** with Anger. You know that it works for you in keeping people in their place.

5. **Self Pity**. All about Self Pity is in the next section of this chapter. At the moment Self Pity means "poor me". Some people don't know that they are carrying suppressed and denied Anger. This Anger they expresses as negative judgments of people around them, punishment, with-holding Love, not saying what they are thinking, being Victims and failing at what they do. As a result of this they get to feel sorry for themselves and how badly their lives are going and how no one loves them. And we feel sorry for them. Poor them. "Poor me" is what they are really saying. Anger is a trump card to Self Pity. Sometimes they will attract violence to themselves. This is an out play of their denied Anger reflected back to them. With all this down side comes a feeling of self importance. It's your "worse than" that gives you your identity.

6. **Fear of Loss**—you are afraid that if you recognize your Anger you are going to have to give up things.

    a) Your image of the nice person that you see yourself as being. Once you admit your Anger then you have to admit that you aren't as nice as you think you are.

    b) You will loose control of being able to threaten and manipulate using Anger. This type of control or power is a false power. It is the unfulfilling "lonely at the top" type of power that Monty Burns, in The Simpsons, demonstrates. True power is the ability to act—it is loving and abundant.

    c) A Fear that you would have to give up your friendships because you would have to admit your Anger and people wouldn't like you anymore. Well if that is your type of friend, then you don't need them. This only applies if you are expressing your angry cleanly. Remember that will build friendships. It is not worth destroying your life to keep a friendship.

Suppressing Anger is denying it. Harboring Anger is expressing it over and again so that year's later you are still angry at "so and so" or "such and such" an event. Just the mention of their name will be enough to set you off all over again. The pay offs, your reasons for holding onto the Anger, will be the same with the exception of Fear of loss of loosing your image.

5.3   SELF PITY

5.31   Introduction

Self Pity can be summed up in two words—POOR ME. We've all heard it. There isn't a person who has never said it to themselves. Poor me—why me?

It is a real emotion—it has both positive and negative attributes. It is also a state of mind, a state of being and a mood. You can end Fear and pain (which are also real emotions) but they are not states of being or thoughts. You can stop self punishment and self sabotage because they are not feelings at all—they are actions that you are taking. You can end Martyrhood, Guilt and Victimhood because they are also not real emotions. They have no real or imagined value at all. They are block-ages and have been thought up. You can end shame because it is with causes that are precise. And you can stop feeling not good enough because it is often a mask for much more devastating and real emo-tions. All of them are devices to overcome Fear of loneliness and the absence of Love in your life.

All negativity has its basis in Self Pity. If you can deal with this you are well on the way to dealing with all the other emotions that are predominately negative in their qualities and the blockages of Martyrhood, Guilt and Victimhood.

5.32   What is Self Pity?

Who experiences Self Pity? Everyone, but there are categories—
1. **The Victim**—the hero of the Gothic novel against whom the world stands and who is feeling sorry for himself. He'll tell you how he feels if you ask him.
2. **The Martyr**—the silent sufferer—he performs to an audience and if you don't drag his story out of him then you'll become another of the others against whom he endures.
3. **The Blamer**—who blames everyone for everything that happens to him.
4. **The Struggler**—he works harder than anyone you know does and they want you to know how unappreciated they are.
5. **The Silent Competitor**—he knows (or thinks he does) he can do better. The person who actually does the thing gets the credit but the silent competitor feels he should be getting the credit.
6. **The Savior**—he's unappreciated. "Look how hard I work", "I've taken time out of my life to help you". He occupies an Ego position of "better than". I will use this term a lot when talking about Ego. Better than is a position that is taken where you compare yourself to another.

All of them say "poor me".

5.33   What Are the Causes of Self Pity?

1. **You learned it.** Again it was the usual suspects. Your parents taught you that life is tough. You learned by watching pity being used to cope and live in the adult world. Society teaches struggle and to be a Victim. Government teaches that you are not strong enough to look after yourselves. Teachers are saying it is admirable to suffer "Look at us. We're under paid". Religion teaches pain, suffering and struggle.

2. The **sexual role package** you tend to adopt in adolescence contains the seeds for Self Pity. The male protects but he's harassed and overworked. The female is compliant and suffers in silence.

3. **The Ego** says "let me do it for you. Don't rely on anything". The Ego wants you to be incapable while it runs your life. And rather than face responsibility and grow up you take the easy road and hand your life to your Ego.

4. **Denial** bleeds into your reality as Self Pity.

5. If you revert back to **childhood or adolescent states of mind**, behaviors will be replayed and that will be enough to produce Self Pity.

6. **Fear of responsibility**.

7. **It's comfortable**. You enjoy it. You can manipulate through weakness. It gives you a nice reassuring feeling to feel comfortable with its familiarity.

5.34   What Are the Ramifications of Self Pity?

- struggle,
- blaming,
- judging,
- rationalizing,
- you feel scared and out of control,
- people don't like you,
- you become fodder for those stuck in the "I am better than" of Ego,
- you never create sustained success,
- you create false and empty personal growth,
- you feel its OK to use Self Pity to manifest your world,
- you end up feeling like a powerless child projecting mother on all woman, father on all men and resenting the world and everyone in it.

5.35   Why Do You Feel Self Pity?

1.   **Habit**—you were born with it or your parents taught it to you.

2.   **Childhood was too painful**—shame based parents dumped it on you. Your parents were totally inadequate. You did not have the vocabulary or feelings to know what was going on. You couldn't leave—you had limited choices. Some died. You could have gone insane or become autistic but you choose to do Self Pity as an anesthetic to numb the pain. You were aware of your destiny and took Self Pity. Drugs and alcohol were also escapes. If you are robbed of childhood then the world is too real for you. Also if adolescence is taken away you turned to pity for the world was too real.

3.   In other cases its what you do when **overwhelmed.** It also means that you do not want to change. It is a manipulation not a legitimate feeling.

4.   It is a **defensive measure**—so instead of dealing with something they went into pity. "I hate (whatever)", therefore not being perfect, they went into pity.

5.   Others come to Self Pity by **embarrassment**—"I'm embarrassed. I'd hate to think that I could do those kinds of things, oh, poor me". From these came your Original Pattern.

Your Original Pattern is the source of your Self Pity. Where did it come from? For example, "they didn't Love me, they did not understand me." At the time it was a viable answer to turn to Self Pity to get through a period, which you may not have otherwise survived. But it is no longer applicable. But you are not doing that now. It is no longer too real etc. You can re-work or edit the past. Being embarrassed is an Ego's position that you no longer have to hold. As you pretend that what began is still true, you have to nobleize it. Now you must look beyond that to find what is real—"that's why I did it then and that's why I pretend I'm doing it now".

5.36   Why Am I Doing Self Pity?

1. Because you desire to be **numb**. It is an anesthetic but all anesthetics cut you off from all your feelings/real emotions. Pity numbs Fear as well as happiness. You are unable to feel anything except Self Pity. Particularly where any feeling of depth of sincerity is involved, pity will numb it. So you are like a zombie.

2. Others desire **blindness**. They do not want to see what they have created in their reality or the world around them. Self Pity is like poking yourself in the eye.

3. To **punish**. You make them feel Guilty, wrong, inadequate, rip away at their sense of Self Esteem, shred their sense of masculinity or femininity, their sense of rightness or their ability to do anything—their sense of power.

    Who has hurt you? And is it not someone who was also in Self Pity? Those who want to punish use Self Pity. They do not know it because they are blind and numb.

    Self Pity is a mechanism for control. We use it to keep people in our reality.

4. You are **arrogant**. You want to be better than. You believe that you don't have to change but that other people should for no other reason than you are better than they are. You are above it all. So it is an excuse that turns to stagnancy and that if untreated can kill you.

5. You desire to be **non-responsive**. You don't want to be responsible. You want the benefits of spirituality but don't want to be spiritual. You feel so sorry for yourself that you have to create your own reality.

6. You **don't want to change**. You want to stay the same. It is an Ego position that comes from Fear.

There is nothing noble about these reasons.

All the reasons as to why you do Self Pity are the effects that it has on you—because you are numb it numbs you, because you are blind it blinds you, and so on with punishment, arrogance and non responsiveness. It is a life style of pain and struggle.

5.4   MARTYRHOOD & VICTIMHOOD

Martyrhood and Victimhood have no redeeming positive qualities at all. They are not emotions but they affect us emotionally. They are a form of self punishment and an emotional blockage. They have their basis in Fear.

5.41   What is Martyrhood?

1. It is **a form of Self Pity and self importance**. Self Pity is a form of self importance anyway. It is more sophisticated than Victimhood and blind superiority, more damaging to you and others and you can't see it as readily.
2. It is **characterized by a number of feelings**—being misunderstood, unappreciated, hopeless, burdened with unbelievable demands, saddled with unsolvable problems, innocent of all responsibility, judged and treated wrongly.
3. Martyrs **live for exoneration in the future**, e.g. "when I finally get to do it my way, then you'll see, I'll be exonerated". But it is always in the future. "You'll see" is one of their favorite phrases.
4. Martyrhood is **silent and righteous Anger that seeks silent and righteous revenge**. It is hostile, not benign. The revenge is based on silent and righteous blame and judgment.
5. Martyrs are **cowards**. They won't say what is wrong for fear of them not being right! They attack from behind afraid of interacting and dealing with reality. There is nothing noble about Martyrhood. Martyrs tend to quickly cut off the conversation. They set booby traps to lure you in.
6. Martyrs are **never wrong**! "I never said that". "I know I never would have said that." "You misunderstand what I said." They will lie in your face.

7.   They **never have impact on anyone else**. All the impact happens to them, e.g. they write off your car and say, "I'm the one with the problems now". A Martyr hurts you, insults you, does damage to you—"look what I'm doing, I'm just so terrible to me."

8.   Martyr is based on a denial of Love. It fuels feelings of powerlessness and is based on a desire to manipulate others through pretending to be weak. It promotes pity and incites Anger and resentment. Your self-image then reflects insecurity with the result that your attitude is one of self-criticism. You sacrifice your integrity and freedom and betray yourself in order to satisfy others. It's not a good look.

5.42   What is Victimhood?

Victims blame. It is a hallmark of being a Victim. "You did it to me" is what they say. Being in Victim is a state that reflects suffering. It supports a position of helplessness and hopelessness. Because this is a planet of free will, you can't be at the mercy of your reality unless you choose to be. But that is choosing anyway, so you can't get away from being responsible for your reality. When you play the Victim you are angry at the other and resent them as you assume a position of inferiority. This resentment or stored Anger leads to disease, e.g. a cancer that eats you away or HIV. These sufferers see themselves as Victims, e.g. a Victim of AIDS. Those words were actually used within the gay community to describe the disease. As a Victim you believe on a deeper level that your circumstances are getting at you, but because you create your own reality, it is actually you who is punishing you.

You could blame someone. Here are some reasons why you would do that—

1.   you hurt me
2.   you didn't' try
3.   you didn't do anything to try and make the relationship work
4.   you rejected me physically, emotionally, spiritually, mentally
5.   you rejected my Love
6.   you rejected the relationship at its very essence

7. for the type of dark Shadow that you have
8. for playing out that Shadow
9. for not being the spiritual wonderful person that you held out the promise of being
10 you let me sleep with you and took my Love, warmth, caring, concern and didn't give back any gratitude
11. you didn't express how you felt
12. you used me selfishly
13. because I am depressed and sad
14. you left me alone
15. you didn't comfort or nurture me
16. you didn't share any of your vast experience with me
17. you wouldn't let me touch you
18. for disappointing me
19. for blaming me
20. for leading me on
21. for not being honest with me in the beginning
22. for not feeling
23. for 14 of the most boring days in my life
24. for the wasted time and effort
25. for throwing away a chance at happiness
26. for not being in touch with your emotions
27. for not being there for me
28. for not taking the next step with me
29. for not being open
30. for using me
31. for hurting me
32. for rejecting me
33. for being competitive
34. for failing
35. because it didn't work
36. for not being attainable
37. for wasting yourself
38. for not understanding me

39. for your lack of compassion
40. for separating yourself from me
41. for not falling in Love with me
42. because as a result I got ill
43. because I am angry
44. for not ever having fallen deeply in Love
45. for being sexually hung up
46. for being a bastard
47. for being hard, selfish, uncaring, tough

In all these cases though you are talking about yourself. You need to start owning that. The Work of Byron Catie can help you enormously here. In a relationship it's never about them. It is always about you. If you can start here then you can change your life for the better. I've never seen this approach fail.

Like Martyr, you are manipulating others through weakness and seek pity to control. Victim enforces the belief of sacrifice in a world of limited resources. It's not a good look either. And it's very boring for those around you too. The opposite of being in Victim is being in your POWER. Power is the energy directed by your will. It lets you generate and transform your reality. It is the antidote to disease.

5.43   The Differences Between Victim & Martyr

VICTIMS	MARTYRS
Feel sorry for themselves. They know it and will tell you for as long as you will listen.	They feel sorry for themselves but will deny it with looks of incredulity until the World ends.
Feel misunderstood, helpless, burdened etc. but will tell you and anyone else who will listen about their problems.	Feel misunderstood etc. but will not admit it and will show you even though they deny it, e.g. "I'm not misunderstood, they didn't hear me right", or "I'm not unappreciated, they didn't have a chance to really know how great I am" or "its my lot in life".
Want you to do it for them and will let you try until you are weary because Victims LOVE to see you struggle—they never suffer. That makes a Victim happy. They will take every suggestion you make and implement it to the letter and fail, come back and tell you it didn't work—it may have even got worse.	Martyrs want you to do it for them, but won't let you help and will fight you at every turn. Martyrs know everything. They want you to do it for them behind their backs so that they do not have to be grateful! They ignore suggestions, say its been done then sneak off and do it. They won't give credit for help. They enjoy your suffering. They never suffer. They are surrounded by the layers of armor of being misunderstood, hopeless etc., justifying and handling most of their dirty work in silence.
Will run from responsibility and admit it. "Terrible me" they will moan and groan.	They feel that they have too much responsibility especially if it is not theirs. They will rush towards responsibility with all kinds of promises and desires for the future. "I'm going to do ... but I have to ..." They are never responsible for other people's responsibility and use that as an excuse for not taking their own responsibility, i.e. "I was busy". It is their favorite game. They stand their ground and refuse in silence. At most they will sigh. MARTYRS LOVE TO SIGH. The more you stamp your feet, the more they like it. Their Anger makes them defiant.

They will use Guilt to lure you in, to get you closer—come and help me; it will never work of course, then they can punish you by saying "it is now worse". Then they are happy.	They won't lure you in but will use Guilt to push you away. They don't want you to point out the Martyrhood nor see it themselves. If you do though they will sabotage you—in the middle of the night if they have to. "Leave me alone. Don't interfere" is their message
They live in the past. "If, if, if ... that had not happened then ..."	They live in the future, e.g. they are polite now because in the future they will be vindicated, e.g. "My Lord is going to come and lift me up ... and you will all go to Hell; then I will be laughing." That is what makes it all right to suffer now. In reality all they really have is their past.
The Victim is a loser and knows it. "Feel sorry for me" they say. They are foolish.	They are also a loser but do not know it. So they are not only foolish but stupid as well. Martyrs believe in winning the future but they never win.

5.44   Why Would You Want To Be A Martyr?

1. **The Grand Promise of the Ego Has Failed**—there has been no unlimited abundance from the Industrial Revolution; and as the promise began to fail, you did not blame your Ego and you blamed human kind. Your Ego promised you happiness when you were freed from the need to survive because of the Agrarian revolution. With the shortage of raw materials you said humanity was greedy and hostile but because you are also part of humanity you would rather destroy yourself than blame your Ego. You blamed the elitists for taking all of the happiness and when you couldn't do all that you wanted to you said that humankind was unloving and that it was the

nature of man to be unloving. You were promised crap and you bought it. Then you blamed humanity for it instead of your Ego. But you did it. You create your own reality. The Ego uses Martyrhood. The characteristics are the same—stupid, self destructive, greedy, hostile, competitive, elitist, unloving. Ego and Martyr are one. You go into Martyr to satisfy your Ego because you'd rather destroy yourself and those around you rather than question your motives.

2.   **The Refusal To Feel Gratitude**—it has been conditioned into you that to feel grateful is weak. Men don't feel gratitude. "It is too vulnerable and people will take advantage of you"—a faulty belief that came from parents. If you are grateful the belief is that you will have to be mean and nasty or people will take advantage of you. But more importantly you won't be able to continue to suffer and you might be loved and feel other feelings like happiness and joy. You may have to admit that there is someone out there nicer than you and that they are using their power more effectively than you. The faulty belief keeps you acting out of Fear.

3.   **You are Holding Onto A Fantasy** that you will never talk of. A fantasy of your grandeur, greatness, of what you will become one day when you are allowed to have the chance to live your life without all these burdens and responsibilities and problems. This fantasy is a lie. You know that it will never happen, you would fail and this is why you do not go after it. And your Martyr keeps calling your bluff. The burdens are excuses that you use not to face the dream. The real reason behind the fantasy is that you want a lot of money so that you can sit back and look at the rest of the World who doesn't have it. So you can watch them suffer AND FEEL BETTER THAN THEM ALL. That is the Ego in action.

4.   **A Greater Power (usually seen as God) Has Done You Wrong,** cheated you somehow and you are angry. You want to punish The Greater Power and you want him to pay but you will never

admit it for Fear of Hell. You are blaming The Greater Power for your actions. Every Martyr in the Catholic Church did something wonderful and was then punished and died dreadfully, suffering. The more suffering the greater the sainthood and the closer you got to The Greater Power. Vindication in the future. The classic example is Jesus on the cross and we have been suffering in the 2000 years that followed. Behind every Martyr there is a Christ complex. It is a fantasy of being Jesus.

5.   Using Martyrhood is **How You Prove You Love**, e.g. that is how mother proved it. "Look how much I am suffering for you." You suffer to prove you Love. "I work this job and I hate it". It becomes a justification, e.g. Love hurts. Therefore the process is self destructive which is of course one of the reasons that some of us do it. WE CHOOSE TO BE A MARTYR. It is self punishing and we are hooked on it.

6.   **You Like Punishing**. It gives you a cheap sense of power. "If I can make you feel less than me, then I become better than you." It is the Ego in action. And if you are better than, then you can say "look how much I have grown" by having compared yourself to the other. Martyrhood lets you hide behind the sweet smile of loving and caring while you turn the knife.

5.5   GUILT

5.51   What is Guilt?

We all talk about it. But what is it really? It has no positive attributes (so therefore it is not an emotion although it affects us emotionally). Make no mistake about that. Don't be fooled by it. It is a form of self punishment created for control and manipulation. It is an emotional blockage that has its basis in Fear. And like all emotional blockages it causes disease and prevents us from receiving Love.

1. Guilt is **Anger that you feel that you have no right to express**, e.g. you may have had to do something for someone but at the time you forgot. They call you to remind you that you forgot. You feel Guilty. But what you are really feeling under that is Anger. Anger at being beholden to that person and Anger at not having done what you were supposed to and you are angry at having it pointed out to you. The Anger is at yourself for not having done something that you should have.

2. Guilt is **an attempt at self control**. You use it to motivate yourself. When you do something out of Fear of getting into trouble, feeling badly or Guilty this is self manipulation. Conscience is a choice based on your principles.

    Guilt is also **an attempt to control others**. So the other person feels terrible or is stopped from expressing how they feel.

3. Guilt is **self punishment looking for purity**. Many on the spiritual path look for cleansing. The self punishment of Guilt is used to burn out the sin, transgression.

4. Guilt is **an attempt to punish others** under the guise of seeking revenge or because of jealousy without admitting that that is what you are doing.

5. Guilt is **a manipulative tool** used in an attempt to make relationships easier but in the end only making them simpler by removing the depth between the people. There is a conflict within us between wanting and not wanting inter-personal relationships. Guilt is used to control the other person making it easier/safer to have a relationship. It is a technique for glossing over the deeper issues which one or both partners do not want to face.

6. Guilt is **a way of denying intimacy**, openness and it keeps relationships shallow. If we are in a relationship and using Guilt to deny our mutual impact then we'll have a simple relationship that is superficial.

7. Guilt is **a paralysis**. It avoids Self Esteem and responsibility. It leads to all physical and emotional inaction.

5.52   What is Guilt Not?

Innocent, cute, sweet, serving of sympathy, noble, clever, your conscience nor uncontrollable. It is a vicious, destructive act to yourself and or others that you have made a decision to take—whether you are aware of it or not.

5.53   Why Do You Feel Guilty?

1. **You learned** to feel Guilty. You were taught by the usual suspects—**your parents**, they were models, e.g. "If you loved me you would…." or "Don't you realize how hard it is for me to…." Society taught you through **school, religion, business** and **government**. The message is someone suffered for you—Jesus, many people, your teachers and parents. Therefore you owe them.

2. It's a **convenient and simple** thing to do.

3. It is a **trump card to Self Pity, control and manipulation** in general. The excuse is that because you feel Guilt then you have the right to be better than, to not be responsible for your actions and therefore to have the right to control and to manipulate.

4. To **relinquish power and responsibility**. Because you feel Guilt then you say "don't expect me to take responsibility". You are really feeling afraid of power. It overwhelms you but it is easier to feel Guilt than it is to deal with power and so you let someone else do it for you.

5. **Ego** and your Fear of your Ego. Your Ego wants to stay in control of you and your life so it uses Guilt to maintain that control. You use Guilt as camouflage to hide its acts. Because of the Ego's position (one of always being better than or worse than what it is comparing you to), e.g. "I'm worse than" lets the Guilt make you feel "better than".

6. When you are out of balance. Guilt is **a stabilizer**. It is familiar, well worn, comfortable ground.

5.54   What Happens When You Feel Guilty?

1. **You get stuck**—you can't decide, act, make choices and consequently you can't move. That forces you to retreat into childhood and adolescent patterns and fantasies so that in turn you create a projection of a critical parent. Your beliefs re-create the projection. Re-living the situation creates more Guilt, paralysis, inertia, projection and you get stuck. It's a vicious circle. It's a lack of creativity, of will and creative imagination and will lead to stagnation.

2. It **keeps you and your life shallow**, boring and you become numb to anything going on.

3. It **fosters Victimhood and Martyrhood**. Poor me.

4. It **leads to resentment, Anger and punishment**. You will eventually punish the object of the Guilt and resent and be angry at it either covertly or overtly.

5. **Leads to physical ailments**, e.g. cancer.

6. It **keeps the past and the pain alive**. These are past and no longer exist. Reality only occurs in the Now so you deprive yourself of living in the moment—the only place where Love lives.

7. **Justifies**—the Ego's position of being better than.

5.6   NOT FEELING ANYTHING AT ALL

It is very painful to be numb and not feeling. It cuts out pleasure and a creative rewarding career, relationship and life. In fact it is like living in a two dimensional world of black and white. There is no color or depth to an experience. It's just like acting or going through the motions. It means nothing. Having lived in that world for most of my life I developed a great working intellect, sharp memory and an ability to problem solve but I never felt a sunset, the color of flowers, empathy, compassion, Love and I never knew if I was in Love. Fear of childhood and adolescent pain kept me detached from feeling anything. And I had emotional blockages to keep me that way alternating between Victim and Martyr while the Shadow of my denial got bigger and bigger behind me tripping up my reality more and more.

So apart from the blockages there are also those behaviors and stimulants that you think are making you feel good whereas in fact they are only keeping you feeling nothing—that is, numb to your feelings. These include red meat, alcohol, nicotine, drugs, chocolate, caffeine and sugar on a chemical level and addictions and compulsive behaviors, e.g. work, gym, sex, shopping, washing your hands, excessively anal retentiveness, anything that is compulsive, that you must do or have. It can be anything, occupying your thoughts and not letting you go. McDonalds, Burger King, Hungry Jacks and all those like them provide plenty of red meat, chocolate, caffeine, sugar and fat. That is why they are so popular. McDonalds and the similar companies are giving the people what the people want—fast, cheap, legal and easily obtained anesthetics. When people wake up and stop demanding this stuff then McDonalds etc. as we know, it will close down, just as cigarette companies are now beginning to pay for the damage that they have been doing to the buyers of their products. In time the alcohol industry is going to be held responsible too. Like in the war against cigarettes, issues of personal safety and health will be how the anti-alcohol lobby will move on government and the industry. Everything in moderation is OK. It is when you let it control you—when you have given your power over to it—that it is a danger to your growth and therefore your enjoyment of life. As the need for addictions cease though there will be a gradual movement away from these agents. That is already happening in the new health conscious world.

Or the numbing to your feelings could come from living in blame, manipulation, justification, Victim, Martyr, Guilt or Self Pity. All the same, some people would rather die from their addictions than face the pain that it subdues.

Often it is too painful to feel. The pain comes from the lack of Love in your lives, the loneliness, the pain of being different, the pain of being rejected, or of not being good enough, pretty enough, built enough, in the right circle enough, rich enough and all the other "enoughs" that you suffer whenever you compare your self to someone or something else. Whenever you buy into comparison and competition you suffer—even by your Ego telling you that you are not good enough or knowing that one day you will be not good enough. No one stays on top forever in the world of illusion. Of course you are good enough. Everyone is. But you have to believe it. The deeper you go into Consciousness the more you move away from the Ego that exists to separate you in the conscious state and into the state that sees us all as being just extensions of deeper levels of energy that are connected. There is nothing wrong with Positive Ego—the Ego that gives you your identity—it is the Negative Ego that is trying to destroy you by making you special that you have to watch.

All addictive or obsessive behavior is a form of self punishment. Self punishment is not letting yourself feel. If you can't feel then you can't feel the desire necessary to create the reality that you want to create. The tools for reality creation are described in Chapter 2.

The pay off with the obsession is that you do not have to accept responsibility. The addiction is the self punishment and that usually brings up shame, which indicates to you that you deserve to be punished. All of this is a smoke screen to what is going on in your thoughts. This is where disease is really coming from.

Chapter 6

—THE MENTAL BODY

It is worth referring to what I said earlier in the introduction to this Division of the Book and in the final paragraph of Chapter 4.

At the sub-atomic level (which is light remember) the thought of the scientist observer has been known to influence the movement of the particles and affect the outcome of the experiment. In other words if the scientist expected a particular result from his experiment then he got it. So if you believe that "such and such" is the cure for something then if the energy is right it will be. Science now undertakes double blind experiments to overcome this problem. Metaphysicians have always said that thought energy creates reality, including our bodies. The question here then is whose thoughts are keeping us in place? Ours or those of the higher frequency of energy that created the field which in turn asks the question "who am I?" At our most fundamental we are holograms of light held together by thought energy. This is the new paradigm or model of thought that is emerging in the West. This new model has major implications when we look at healing and how it is thought that makes us; and more importantly, how you use thought to create your own reality. If thought can affect the cellular structure, then does the idea of mind over matter, the power of positive thinking and creative visualization have some credence in science? Yes it does if you adhere to the new model. These open up new avenues for reality creation and self healing.

It is a function of the Mind or Mental Body to try to understand the world and during our lives we have developed a framework or structure or some reference in our Mental Body to do that job. All information or stimulus that is received by our five senses is interpreted through this framework. It is how we make sense of the world. This is why each of us can see the same event and have a different experience of it. This frame work through which we understand the world is called our belief system. Our beliefs—or the way we see the world—have been acquired from other people and sources of information. We then have taken these as our own beliefs. They have been acquired from the usual suspects—our parents, our families and their friends, our schooling, our peers, the church, the government, the media. As well as from other sources such as libraries, pop culture, your community, sub-culture, and genetics. Some would also say from past lives or you brought them in when you incarnated into this reality. Create a new belief system and you change your perception and therefore your experience of what happens. The world is just what you think it is. The reality of perception is that it is neither right nor wrong. It is just perception. It is right for me. Yours is right for you. It is subjective and therefore valid—the issue is does your perception serve you in you becoming more of who you are in you growing into a happier, more balanced person who is successful?

So the old saying—it's all in the Mind—has never been more true.

Our experiences are determined by our beliefs—these beliefs first showed up as our experiences of childhood, from adolescence, our experiences of being successful and of having failed. Various people have categorized our beliefs from coming from different aspects of which we were in the past. For example when ever we are demanding that we are not getting enough then we are said to be in our "child" aspect of our consciousness. And behaviorists might argue that this when a person is put into a situation then that is sufficient to produce a similar or identical reaction to the one that was first experienced under those conditions. Continual exposure to the stimulus then reinforces the behavior.

It is useful then, from the point of view of understanding the various aspects of us from which our beliefs are sourced, to recognize these various aspects.

I have previously referred to there being different aspects of psyche. These include the Ego (both in its positive and negative senses), the child, the adolescent, your adult, the Mask, the Idealized Self Image, the Shadow, the Future Self, the Lower Self, the Real Self and the Transcendent Self as the major aspects. All of these are in the Mental Body. So therefore they are just thoughts though—vibrations of energy that impact on our vibrational bodies which resonate at slower frequencies, i.e. the Emotional Body, the Etheric Body and the Physical Body. Analysis of the Mental Body into various aspects merely lets us label them so that they become tangible for us to deal with.

An understanding of the roles of the aspects makes it easier for you to identify where you may be coming from when you find yourself stuck in your head with thoughts going round and round or "bad" or fearful things happening to you. Then you can take steps to rectify it so that you regain control of who you are and correct what damage may have been done while you were in that aspect of your psyche. Eventually you can be aware all the time—when you attain that state that is called being an adult.

I have selected the Ego and the Shadow as the major aspects to look at. There are others, such as the creations (or identities) that we have made from these, e.g. the social mask that we wear when we meet people for the first time, the idealized self image we have of our selves, i.e. the image of how we would like to see ourselves and which we project onto the person whom we want as a partner, friend or to be with in a relationship.

The bottom line is that they are all just thoughts anyway. As human consciousness we are moving beyond labeling and beginning to see a bigger picture now—one more like the one put forward by this book.

6.1   THE EGO

6.11   Introduction

Unless otherwise noted when I talk about Ego generally here I am talking about the positive and the Negative Ego as a singular collective aspect of the Mental Body. The Outer World that you experience with your five senses is the world as experienced by your Conscious Mind as delivered to you by your Ego so that you can make sense of the world you are sensing. It is the world you experience when you are awake. Most people think reality starts and stops here. As a consciousness you developed an aspect of yourself through which to receive and transmit the data or content of your Outer World into your Conscious Mind. The Conscious Mind takes the images and gives it form and a context in which to understand and interpret the information. This is the role that the Ego enjoys the most. Information concerning your reality. That aspect of you is called your Ego. You can't kill your Ego. It is part of your Energy System. If it dies—you the human being dies. If you want to change it, it needs to be released or busted. If threatened, it will do everything that it can to survive—even if it means killing you—so be careful because it plays tricks all the time to ensure its survival and to get what it wants—think of the movie Gremlins. Starts off nice but gets bad.

The most immediately recognizable aspect of our Mind is our Ego—that aspect of us that makes each of us different from the rest. Many other aspects exist, and each of these have their own role in determining who we have become as well as us having determined who those aspects are. It is a two way street.

6.12   Egoic Development

To understand Ego you need to understand how it came to be what it is now. Ego develops in 3 stages. **The Infant Ego** emerges between ages birth and 7-14 years. Here its concern is "am I getting enough?", e.g. sleep, food, Love, toys, space. Quantity is sought.

The Image Based Ego arises from ages 7-14 to 21 and asks "Am I good enough?" Look at teenagers. "Is my house, the clothing I wear, my parent's looks, my father's job, my car, my friend's social position…good enough?". It is the age of embarrassment when teenagers are ashamed of their families. Everything is image. It's all or nothing at this age. "I could just die of embarrassment when my mother arrived at the dance". A time of extremes and absolutes.

The Exploring Ego which develops between 14-21 and grown up is concerned with "Am I learning enough?", e.g. "am I advancing enough in my career, growing as a person enough, changing enough, keeping up with it all enough?".

Somewhere between grown up and spiritual adult you reach the Positive Ego which says "I am enough" and you get a sense of harmony and of being complete while becoming more. But at this point you could stagnate in one of the Ego positions, e.g. a physical adult stuck in child will take the biggest piece of pie whether or not they need it. Or the physical adult stuck in adolescent who buys a new car every year for status reasons—"am I good enough". And the physical adult who gets 3 university degrees because his Ego is asking him "am I learning enough". Once you begin to understand that people do things from Ego it makes it harder to judge them for doing these things. You just accept them for what they are. It is the Ego that Loves to judge and thereby separate you even further, alienating you even more from your world. Once you recognize what aspect of Ego you are coming from it is easier to start making choices from a freer and less driven basis.

What is it that goes wrong to make the Ego go negative? As you get older and you learn to cope in the world you start to give your Ego the responsibility of delivering the context of the information in your world. In many ways it is a laziness that creeps up on you—you aren't even aware that it is happening—most people never know that it has happened and stay stuck in a Fear based reality. It is already delivering the content of the information to you. So it now not only delivers the information but it analyses it too. That is not its job. That is the job of your rationalization. So with the added work load it doesn't have time to mature, it is not equipped to do the work. So it does it poorly and fails. It starts faking it (the Ego then takes what it knows and dreams and fantasizes of what it can't deliver). It promises everything and delivers nothing—ever. Then, because of information overload, it gets angry at you for giving it a job it can't do, and finally it starts to see you as the enemy, as well as the world that it can't deal with. This is the impetus for the destructive elements of humanity to emerge. It is distorted male energy—control, domination. This is the Ego that I shall speak of from now on. The Negative Ego.

At this stage your Ego replaces the roles of your Subconscious Self, your Unconscious Self and your Higher Self and interprets it all. These are also vibrating energy bodies that exist at the Mental Body level of your Energy System and beyond. As it takes over your thinking and interpretative process everything becomes the enemy and it has to control everything that comes into and goes out of your Mind. At some point you decide that as your Ego is not mature, wise, smart and is still failing, that you will kill it. So it now sees you as the enemy and so it decides to kill you before you can kill it. This becomes its primary function so it now always lies to you. Always. It never keeps its promise. It is always wrong. It is too stupid to realize that without you then there is no it.

But by now you have become co-dependent with your Ego. I'll give you an example of how a co-dependent Ego works. Someone knocks over a vase in your home. Your response is to buy another. Your Ego says "they did it on purpose because they don't like you, so wait until you are at their house then accidentally break something of theirs". The Ego casts doubts which eat away at you planting seeds in your Mind that slowly eat you away. The Ego lays down strict rules (a co-dependency criteria) and this diminishes your capacity to Love, e.g. when you meet someone you are all thumbs and it says "you can do better, use them to get someone better". Ego is all about control. You neglect your Ego (a co-dependency criteria) and made a rule that it manages your life.

6.13   Origins of the Negative Ego

1. **When you do not think**—we are taught by the usual suspects—parents, school, society, government, religion, and a stubbornness to stay in the past, not to think. When you don't think then your Ego has to. It is easy not to think—TV programs that draw the conclusion for you and home entertainment make you a sponge. This makes you vulnerable. It is no longer possible to know everything. Once you could. Now with so much knowledge this further discourages thinking. So the problem of Ego is bigger than it used to be and is getting bigger all the time. This overwhelming knowledge means that you have to learn to ask for help now instead of relying on your Ego—but you don't ask for the help. Remember that it is the Ego acting through Fear that is the basis of disease. It is the Ego that separates and causes powerlessness.

2. **People are more and more reluctant to grow up**—"I feel 18", "school days were the best days of your life". If this is so, you are not accepting your adulthood. Your Ego has taken over your Mind and you are living in the past.

3. **The Fear of responsibility & accountability**—never wanting to make a mistake is a Fear. Society is moving faster and faster now so it is scarier to make a mistake. A little mistake 50 years ago could be a big mistake now. Noticed how much faster time is passing? When you look for the quick answer this lets the Ego in.

4. **Not accepting that you create your own reality**—society says that you are at the effect of your reality and that you are powerless against it. This lets the Ego in.

5. **You don't Love yourself or others or you won't forgive yourself or others**—this devours your brain and then the rest of

you until there is only a shell living in a grand illusion created by the Ego.

6. **Fear of loneliness**—with your Ego talking to you in the back of your head you'll never be lonely. You will always have it to talk to.

6.14   The Messages of the Ego

These are

1. I can do it all by myself—I don't need anyone (a cause of AIDS—defensiveness).
2. Somebody else has to do it for me.
3. I am the best—I am the worst: it is always one extreme or the other—all comparisons of best are made from a place of Ego.
4. I am evolved, there is nothing more that I have to learn—I am so un-evolved, I couldn't possibly learn.
5. I always make mistakes, I can never do anything right, I am perfect.

Ego always comes from extremes.

There are certain characteristics that tend to show that the statement is an Ego statement.

They **deal with specialness** as opposed to uniqueness either covertly or overtly, e.g. good/bad statements.

1. They tend to **justify and rationalize rather than take responsibility** and understanding. This includes explanations. If your first response is an excuse it is usually coming from Ego.
2. They tend to **deny rather than to accept**.
3. They are **blaming statements rather than loving statements**, e.g. I am leaving you for your own good. They can be punishing statements, usually subtle. It is not so much the words but the thoughts that you are thinking.

Reflecting Ego are the states of distraction (you can't focus), contempt, unreliability (being irresponsible) and failure (which come from believing in being inferior).

The opposite of Ego is Mastery. This is the ideal that we seek in healing ourselves. It is what allows us to operate as a Supreme Being in perfect harmony with the Universe that we seek to return to as part of our evolution of consciousness. In many ways the Universe is like the main frame of a computer in which you are a networked laptop. When in harmony there can be no disease. A Master knows that he has the power to create it all and that he is responsible for his actions.

6.15   The Impact of Ego

When in Ego you are in Fear—plagued by self-doubt and obsessed by a fraction of which you really are. Most people are stuck in Ego most of the time—unless they are coming from those other aspects called child or adolescent. It is also called being insecure. Being in Ego is giving your Ego your power and therefore you become powerless. This powerlessness leads to illness because it is imbalance.

Ego is the tyrant, Victim and punisher all in one. It is your enemy. It will kill you. Ego loves to judge and criticize—and it is never enough. Whenever you judge/criticize you give Ego control. It seeks to control you all the time. It is the yamma yamma that hammers away in your head incessantly never letting up, cajoling you, belittling you, making you insecure, fooling you, playing on your Fears, chipping away at your Self Esteem and power. Ego destroys its creator—the thing that it serves. You can't bargain with it, e.g. HAL in 2001 represented the Ego.

The Ego creates alienation and causes struggle and conflict for you in your life. It separates you from truth impeding your ability to Love and therefore to heal yourself, to be who you really are and to let you have what you really want. It never goes away because nothing can be destroyed—only ever changing shape.

So this is the danger of being "in Ego". It is a game of Russian roulette that you can't win. To heal you must get your Ego out of the way. To escape from it is your first step to freedom and represents the lifting of a great weight from your shoulders, removing the blinkers from your vision and of you taking back your power.

6.2 CONSCIOUSNESS

Memories are stored in the body. Beliefs are stored in consciousness.

6.21 The Subconscious.

It is like a data bank, storing everything that the body experiences. Even all those events and sensations that you may not even be aware of, e.g. your heart beating, your eyes blinking, everything you have ever sensed. It is a faithful servant programmed exactly like software, never questioning nor judging. Just performing. You create the situations and it responds as programmed.

Your Sub-conscious is thinking all the time. Sending out the information on how to act and respond—directing you by remote control with pre-programmed tapes and sometimes you are doing it and not even aware of the pattern. Your Sub-conscious talks to you in dreams using symbols. Your Sub-conscious is creating your reality for you so you need to know what is in it. That is where some of your beliefs are stored and it is where you go when you dream.

Your Sub-conscious has the ability to communicate with the Sub-conscious of other people. Thought is energy. The energy of your thoughts can be heard by the subconscious of the other person. It is like transmitting radio waves. Inaudible to the ear but perceptible to the right receiver. This explains why you can sometimes tell if a person is lying or what they are actually thinking. It is also called intuition. Your Sub-conscious resides in the solar plexus—hence the term "gut feeling". Often you will know things on a Sub-conscious level but not know of it on a conscious level or know it but not know why. This is why. So the Ego not only hurts you it also hurts others with its judgments. You always have impact on other people even if you are only just thinking about them.

6.22   The Unconscious.

On a deeper, or more correctly, a higher vibratory level, beyond your Sub-conscious, is your Unconscious Mind. It is here that there resides your deepest Fears and most hidden desires. It is where there resides your "so called" Dark Side. The deeply hidden truths about the you that only you know and don't know. The part of you that you do not want anyone to see. That is why some of you are so afraid of intimacy and commitment. One night stands and having affairs not longer than a few weeks—even hiding behind the Internet. It is within the Unconscious Mind that you hold the bulk of your beliefs. All beliefs that you share with others reside here, e.g. the world is round, the sun rises in the east, the color we call blue is the color blue, airplanes fly, death is certain, we live so long as we breath, antibiotics work (although the shared belief now is that they may not although that has more to do with the nature of disease than with the effectiveness of drugs—but that's another story). It is these beliefs that connect all human beings. Within the Unconscious are the beliefs of the mass consciousness. And they exist whether we are consciously aware of them or not. They are continually running and emitting out of us into the world. So your Unconscious Mind is also creating your reality with its beliefs. Imagine how much energy that there must be present if everyone on the Planet shares them. That is why when everyone on the planet thinks the same thing at the same time that it is possible to actually change perception and reality. The energy generated by large groups of people is potent.

Remember in the first *Star Wars* movie when Obi One is talking to Luke and suddenly he stops as though he has just heard something and he turns to Luke and says "I feel that there has been a great movement in the Force as if a million voices have been silenced in a singe scream" (well, words to that effect anyway), and he feels the death of those people who have been vaporized by Darth Vader's weapon of mass destruction (the Death Star)? Obi One was so highly tuned into the Force (rhymes with Source—which is another name for God, Universe etc.) that he was aware of a disturbance within it. Most human beings are not that aware. If a thousand people die in an earthquake in China we don't know about it until we see the news. We have not only cut our connection with the Force but we have also numbed out to our feelings that are the connectors to our deeper levels of consciousness.

The more conscious you become, the more you connect with your feelings, the more intuitive or psychic you become, and the more you connect to the deeper aspects of how the world works and what it really is. It is a heightened state of awareness. Love is a state of awareness and the more heightened your awareness the more in a state of Love you are. The more aware you are the less judgmental, the more connected and the more happy you are as you connect more directly into a state of higher vibration and Love.

Fears will still come up but you will deal with them efficiently and quickly. They will no longer run your life. That it what spirituality is all about. If you are connected at this level then you are no longer denying your connection with the Universe and spending your life staying numb so that you can't connect with deeper aspects of who you are. For many people that is why they are so empty, and why life is so meaningless. It is because they are not connected with the deeper aspects of who they are. They are just their conscious waking selves living in the world that they see—hence the term they are asleep led by their guide dog—their Ego. When you connect you will have let go of the behaviors in your life that you think you were enjoying (or may be unaware of) but which are really keeping you stuck in old patters, numb to feeling alive and unhappy. Habits like smoking will just vanish. You will have let go of the reason to smoke and not been aware of it. In fact it was so easy to do you will wonder why you hadn't done it earlier.

6.3 THE SHADOW

We are all looking to make the right decisions. We all have our own agendas—being loved and accepted are on everyone's and are a prime motivator. So we are always judging the criteria by which to make the choice. So the world works this way—we establish a framework of reference (these are our beliefs, attitudes and values of right and wrong) and judge everything according to it. It is a belief system—a filter system from which we can then make choices and decisions.

Other people may call our choices into doubt because they have a different set of beliefs, attitudes and values of right and wrong. So you will find that like-minded people stick together and like to stick together—you won't find Democrats in the Republican Party. The resonance of energy keeps them that way—at least until their Shadow comes out to face them in the form of people who confront them. So everyone is justifying their own belief system all the time when in fact no one's belief system is right or wrong—as you've seen in Division I, they are always just subjective points of view. Thoughts that have been labeled to give us meanings we are comfortable with. This is, as I have said, a planet of free will. There are no absolutes laid down. Everything is just a point of view. That is why we have laws. To keep peace and to maintain order. But even these are subjective and are only workable when the majority agree to abide by them. In essence the will of the people is reflected in the laws which govern people. Beliefs are a filter system through which action is chosen or denied. The filters being wants, needs, hurts, Fears, hates, Loves, etc.

When you choose one thing you do not choose another. When you have one thought you are not having the opposite of that thought—you are denying it. This is Polarity. For example, you might wish your neighbor dead but because you have been taught that it is wrong to kill (and have therefore taken on the belief that it is wrong) you do not premeditate their death. Instead you push the thought out of your Mind and often with it the feelings of hate or Anger towards them. You deny your urge.

The more time we spend creating a particular pole the more time we spend creating the opposite. Look at politics, the swinging of the pendulum and the way it is reflected in voting trends and in social trends, e.g. the radical parents breeding the conservative children and vice versa. We fight illness and war but we can never win and they never go away. No matter how hard we try. In fact the harder we try the more they come back. The more we nourish one pole the more the other secretly builds up in the shadows where we can't see it—where we don't want to see it. We need to learn to accept both poles as being valid and let them just be. We need to acknowledge that both poles are valid. Continual judging and choosing reinforces our internal division. This internal division will ultimately surface as illness. Illness is a polarity too. The more we try to avoid it the more we are certain to create it. Without illness there can be no curing which is the opposite of it. A healing is something else. A healing is rising above the polarity all together.

But where goes the energy of the thoughts and feelings that you do not want to have or feel that you can't have? What happens to your "non-choice?"

Thoughts are forms of energy. Energy can't be destroyed—only transformed, transmuted or transcended. This denial of thoughts that you do not choose or do not want to have, is stored within you—in your Unconscious Mind—out of sight and out of your conscious awareness, in that part of your awareness that is called your Shadow. The Unconscious is part of your Soul—the part of you that sees an even bigger picture of who you are and where you are going on your journey back to the Universe. Sometimes it steps in with thoughts and creates a reality for you that parts of you would prefer had not happened. It does this where your Ego has caused you to move away from your Soul's purpose. In these cases you just can't be sure which part of you is creating your reality. When you become sufficiently familiar with yourself then you will know that in the absence of all explanation then it is probably your Soul guiding you. It will always be for your highest good if this is the case. How do we know that? Because it is what it is. You can't argue with what is. If you do then you suffer. Accept what is and you will save yourself a lot of pain and suffering.

Shadow was a term coined by Jung to describe that part of ourselves that we preferred not to carry around in our Conscious Minds and that we pushed into the darkest corner of our Mind hoping to forget that it was there. But like a shadow, whilesoever you are in the light, it will always be there behind you. It is only when you are in darkness with your Shadow that you can't see it—but it remains there all the same only now you are right in it. It is part of the intangible you—the inner unseen you. As you change so does it. Peter Pan lost his shadow and had to go in search of it to be complete. It was a woman (Wendy) who sewed it back onto him. The point should not be lost. It was the female energy that was the catalyst for making him complete. Sometimes it is in the simplicity of children's stories, rich with their metaphors, that real truth lies. The children can't see the truth, only the images, but these are stored forever in their subconscious to be activated at some later time when they need to be. For Peter Pan the shadow was the rest of him and for some people it is the best of them, waiting in the shadows of their Minds to be uncovered.

What is happening now in our evolution on the Planet is that the Unconscious (and therefore our Shadow) is becoming conscious (or awareness and part of our reality), and we are being forced to look at ourselves. In that looking at who we are we are also asking what our purpose is on the Planet. On a planetary level we are being called upon to look at what we have denied, e.g. our own destruction of the planet's resources as a by-product of the Industrial Revolution, the disease of cancer caused by the pollution of our bodies with chemicals, the diseases of the heart caused from not being open to receiving and expressing Love and the diseases of herpes, HIV and AIDS, by products of the Sexual Revolution and lack of regard that we have for ourselves as projected by our lack of regard for others.

The Shadow comes with you at birth in the same way that your Ego also does. The Shadow holds all the stuff that you can't deal with at that age—Fear, power, strength, Anger, hurts, abuse, hate, greed, insecurities, talent and anything else you don't want to look at or deal with. Then it gives them back to you to deal with when you get older and are more capable of dealing with them, whether or not you think that you are capable at the time of doing so. From its higher vantage position in your consciousness it knows when you are ready.

Your Shadow is an entity within you. It is not a complex. It never lies to you and is a true ally to you. Its enemy is the Negative Ego. You have mistakenly allied with your Ego believing it to be your friend— it said it was—when the reality is that your Shadow is your friend for that is where your denied power exists. It being a dark and scary place though you are too afraid to face your Fears that live there. By going beyond your Fears you can recover the gold that you have been storing there. For many it is creativity, their voice to speak up, self-confidence, talent, joy for living or sense of deserving.

The Ego knows that and will do anything it can to stop you from accessing your alliance with your Shadow and therefore your denied power. It knows that there lies your ability to do whatever you want to do. You see it takes a lot of energy to hold energy. And you are using a lot of energy to keep those denied feeling and thoughts denied. If you let go of that holding energy and then release the energy you feel or think you shouldn't have it will be like blowing up the dam. You will be flooded with new energy, vitality, aliveness, determination, will power and be freed from having to hold onto that Anger and Fear, which without you knowing is subtly directing your thoughts, feelings, choices, decisions and attitudes. The important point here is that these are the very things that make your life what it is. You do not yet realize how vital these things are to your very existence. Your Ego does though.

The Ego will play on your Fears of the unknown and will create doubt in your Mind to stop you from looking at the Shadow. It knows that its loss of control over you is certain when you align with your Shadow. Remember that the Ego hates change and hates to loose control of you. It will stop you however it can from you taking this next step on your path to self-realization, self-discovery and of you finding out who you are. It wants to keep you in the dark and it uses Fear and apathy to do so. Go back to the Fear section now if Fear is coming up. Command the Fear to leave. Looking at your Shadow entails you giving up part of you—the image built by the Ego. Of you letting go of a familiarity of how you think the World works. It involves giving up the way of the Negative Ego. It is Fear that you feel when facing this new part of yourself. Part of the reason for this is that you have stored in your Shadow most of the Fear that you are unaware. By refusing to face your Shadow you retard your growth and sabotage your progress. You remain blocked by your own resistance. Self Love heals the scars that are hidden in the Shadow and restores your life force, bringing renewed vitality. Love is fully discussed in the next chapter.

Your Shadow stands between who you think you are (your idealized self) and who you really are (your true self). You need to make peace with your Shadow. It is a very important and big step. After working with my Shadow my whole life began to change. New opportunities for being who I really was opened up. The more I demonstrated my desire to find out who I was the better life became. In this process of healing I took back my power.

Shadow work is one of the most important areas of your awakening to who you really are. It may also be one of the most confronting because in the Shadow you have to look at that part of yourself that you do not like and have not acknowledged exists within you, e.g. the mean, nasty vengeful and bitter person that you sometimes feel you are. It is the part of you that believes that you are not worthy. The part that won't let you have an intimate loving relationship. The part of you that you do not want others to see in Fear that they may not like you. So you deny the intimacy with them. Within it lies the motivation of much of who we are. Beyond it lies the true self—the one who is free to choose. This is where you want to be. Free to choose. Not having to choose because you are afraid. Once you find yourself truly free to choose you will wonder why you didn't do it earlier. It is such a great place to be.

To find out who you are, you have to have a good hard look at all of you. It is the first step in accepting all of who you are. If you accept all of who you are then there is no denial energy at work surreptitiously working away in your underworld influencing you to make a world for yourself which will satisfy it when you could be making a world to satisfy you. Within your Shadow you carry the denial of your homosexuality if you are heterosexual and vice versa. If too denied then it will erupt as it did for instance in the 2000 Academy Award winning movie for Best Picture, Best Actor and Best Original Screenplay *American Beauty*. And if that wasn't a true enough reflection of society then see Hilary Swank in the 2000 Academy Award Winning movie for Best Actress—*Boys Don't Cry*. Even *Easy Rider* (back in the 1970's) had it's own undertone. Here is to be found the Guilt that goes with being different to the rest (and therefore in the Minds of many of you not being good enough—here enters Ego with its better thans and worse thans). In the Shadow is also found the denial of the hate that many of you feel to your parents—of the strong loathing and unforgiveness that you feel towards these people. And if you are saying, "no, I love my parents" then part of you is saying, "I hate them". You are even denying it now!! It is polarity at work—you think that your parents never hated you? Some of you drove them insane with what you used to do. And the denial will not be gone until you go into the Shadow and confront it and make peace with it so that you can have peace within yourself from the torment and self punishment that you put yourself through in your day to day living, failures and not getting what you want.

Whilesoever you continue to blame it stops you from loving yourself and being healed of the imbalance in your feelings that are stored in your Shadow. When you get into it, Shadow work becomes compelling. The deeper you go into it the more benefit you will see come out of it. You'll start to love it and overcoming the Fear will be liberating and empowering. As you become more in touch with who you really are—as you get rid of the crap out of your Mind and body—you will begin to see very clearly just what the Shadow is—a vault of your energy that you have denied yourself the use of. Therefore it is a source of power to you—an endless supply that you can use whenever you want to. You will not be disappointed in working with your Shadow. It is an imperative. Until you do you will never access your power and you will never know who you really are. And in the end you will just love it—because you will have faced your darkest Fears and found that they can't hurt you. You will thus have opened yourself to the healing power of Love, which you know, is more powerful than Fear. Love is always the answer.

Be aware that if you do not accept that you have your disease and if you do not look squarely at what that means—usually because of Fear—that you are denying this condition that you are in and know that denial energy is stored in the Shadow. And the more you deny it the greater power you give it. The more power it has the greater the likelihood of you experiencing the thing that you are denying e.g. if you have ever given up smoking or tried to, the more you deny the craving for a cigarette the stronger the desire to have one becomes. The following thought worked for me. When you give up anything never tell yourself that you can never have it again. Knowing that you are free to have it again will free you to walk away from it e.g. with smoking say "I choose at this moment not to smoke". Don't say, "I will never have a cigarette again". Your body goes into shock at the thought of being deprived of this drug. Fool it. It can cope with not having a cigarette in this moment if it thinks that it can have one in the next moment. It never gets one of course and eventually it forgets it wants one. It helps if at the same time that you are looking at why you are smoking in the first place. Otherwise you will replace one addiction with another. Notice how fat people can get when they give up smoking? This is why.

As you work with your Shadow you will come to realize that there really is no such thing as good or bad. Darkness or the Dark Side or Blackness that is epitomized so much in horror movies and the viciousness that we see played out in world—either as rape, murder, war, starvation, torture and cruelty—is just denied energy that has festered in the Dark. It isn't right or wrong. It just is. Think about it for a minute. Darkness is the absence of Light. Once light is shone there is no darkness. If you stand in your living room in the day light you can see all that which is around you. At night you can't but those things that you saw in your living room in the daylight are still there at night. By shining light on your Shadow you see what is there, you accept it and move on knowing that it can't harm you again. It is really so obvious when you think about it. Your Fears are in your Shadow. You were too afraid to look at them so you put them in your Shadow. A lifetime of Fears resides there now. No wonder it is scary to look into the Shadow.

It is a Catch-22. The older you get the more Fear you have denied. The more Fear you have denied the scarier life gets as the Fears start to manifest. The more the Fears start to manifest the more that Fear is resisted. So as you get older the less Love you have and the more dis-ease you get.

These Fears stop you feeling worthwhile. They impede your power and Self Esteem. The Shadow can also be called your evil side. The more that you reject or deny aspects of who you are the more power you give it. All that is evil, destructive and negative is a result of defending against experiencing pain. This denial stagnates energy. When feelings stagnate then energy stagnates and if energy stagnates you can't move. You die. The Shadow has to be transformed. It can't be transcended. It is part of your path. Once past it your Fears can never hurt you again. Once past it you are free to allow Love into your life unafraid of it. You see, most people won't let Love in because they know they can't handle it—subconsciously they know what is in their Shadow.

Chapter 7

—THE CAUSAL BODY

Beyond the Etheric, Emotional and Mental Bodies lies the Causal Body. The Causal Body is sometimes called the Higher Self and this is a stepping stone back to even higher frequencies. It is the highly vibrating energetic body that stores the experience of the physical body in all of its incarnations. Reincarnation is a model that says that the higher energies keep creating and energizing matter for the purpose of the matter experiencing life in 3D so that the energy can feel physical matter, acquire knowledge and grow spiritually. Reincarnation explains why life is a learning experience and why we are here. In other words the meaning of life is to learn. The early Christian Church taught reincarnation—Jesus had learned of it in his time in India after the flight to Egypt to escape Herod but for their own political purposes the Roman Catholic Church removed it from its teachings. If we connect with our Higher Self, we can see life from the bigger picture of what we are here to learn, what we have already learned from past lives and where we are going as a consciousness.

Depictions of saint's Etheric energy is represented by a halo of light thus depicting the connection back to the lighter or higher vibration of Source energy or God.

7.1   THE HIGHER SELF

The Higher Self is the part of your consciousness that is constantly in the Light and Love. It has an over-view of you and your life and can see where you have been and where you are going to, without being hampered by having to experience everything that you are—such experiencing making it difficult for you to have the clear perspective that your Higher Self possesses.

A very good book on the subject is *Spiritual Growth: Being Your Higher Self* (printed by H J Kramer Inc in 1989 by Sanya Roman). In terms of personal growth and awareness, for you to connect with your Higher Self will accelerate your growth exponentially and assist you tremendously in dealing with your Fear. Remember it is your Fear that stops you from changing and growing into more of who you really are—your True Self. Disease is only an imbalance in your energy.

Through connecting with your Higher Self you will connect with the great power that is The Universe. Through it you will be able to access if you like what I'll call the Universal Library. That is, all knowledge. The Universal Mind and the Universal Will are there to be accessed as well.

7.2   THE SPIRIT and THE SOUL

These are also aspects of your higher consciousness who are the interface between you and the Universe. They guide you and through their connection to the Unconscious Mind will direct your daily life from their over-viewing perspective. It is their thoughts that you are thinking and these aspects of you will often create a crisis in your life to put you back on track so that you are aligned with your life's purpose and learning your life's lesson. A track that your Ego has led you.

7.3   THE UNIVERSAL MIND,

also called the Universe (a scientist's point of view), All That Is (a New Age term), the Force (from *Star Wars*), the Source without a Source (which is what God means), Christ Consciousness (a revised spiritualist's viewpoint), God (the male polarity and 11th chakra connection) and the **Goddess** (the female polarity and 12th chakra connection). All of these words describe aspects of the same ultimate energy of the Creator—the cause without a cause. It is through these aspects of energy that we are connected ultimately back to the place from where we came. Each aspect has its own function in the process. This then explains today's wider held view that all of us are not only part of all that is but we exist within All That Is or the Universe. I am not going to use the term God because then it won't bring up the Sub-conscious feelings you have from when you heard the religious word God. Most people tune out when they hear it.

Being aware that we are spiritual beings lets us connect with all of who we are and it gives us an anchor that says we are not alone but part of a bigger picture to which we can access anything and everything. And before your Ego starts saying—"yeah, sure"— consider this: have you been willing to have it, has part of you believed that it wasn't possible (for whatever reason) or that you didn't deserve it, or in some way put a limitation on yourself and said "this is how it is and I can't change it. I will never have it. Only they will". Because if you did, you opened the door to the Negative Ego's voice of Self Pity, Victim and Martyr and you then went down the road of Fear to limitation, separation and loneliness. The way home to having whatever you want in your life is connecting with all of who you are. Acknowledging your spirit.

I want you to just take on the thought that you are more than just whom you think you are. I want you to see yourselves in this new light of being a person made up of many different aspects. I want you to see that the earth is more than just the third rock from the sun with plants and animals on it. I want you to see that you are vortexes of dynamic energy. Intricate and alive. Full of light. Because that is where a healing is going to take you. To a higher vibration where the slow vibrations of disease can't reach you. And once there then you can start to receive all the abundance that the Universe always intended that you should have.

By now you will be getting the picture that the further you go inside yourself the more you are going to get the answers as to what is happening on the outside of your life—out there in 3D—in that hologram of light we call planet Earth.

There is a whole Inner World that exists along side the Outer World of the 3rd dimension and the Ego. As enormous and endless as the Universe may appear to be, it is just a capsule of energy accessed by thought and experienced through the senses. What if there was more than one universe and those other universes existed in other dimensions and that these were just part of All That Is? Think about that. And why couldn't it be so? Could deep space just be the Outer World equivalent of the Inner World's Unconscious Mind? The deeper we go into space the more of the Unconscious Mind we will discover? First we find it in the Unconscious Mind then we find it in space. Remember that belief creates reality—so if we believe there is life out there then there is life out there. Eventually science will prove it to be so. Science is seriously now beginning to think that there is more than one universe. *Star Trek* followers already know about them, the children in C. S. Lewis' ***Chronicles of Narnia*** know about them and Physicist Michael D. Lemonick believes they are real too. In fact since the 1950's with the work of quantum mechanics physicist Hugh Everett and later relying on the work of the great Danish physicist Niels Bohr, Stephen Hawking and M.I.T physicist Alan Guth, seriously consider that universes beget universes and that other universes exist—black holes being the portals. Keep stretching the mind and the sphere in which it is trapped—the 3rd dimension— will continue to expand.

You are not just a person in a human body but much more. An identity with a connection to the Universe. Someone who belongs and who is never alone. Therefore you always have access to unconditional and unlimited Love and knowledge through your internal connections to the Universe.

So let's go back to the old question "what came first—the chicken or the egg?" In other words was it the DNA or the environment that produced the genius or the monster? I believe that DNA responds to the environment. Having now seen the model of the energy systems that forms the human you can see why DNA is the product of consciousness and that it is consciousness and the light of the Universe that fuels it, that creates the environment through you. This is now being supported scientifically by people such as Professor Robert Sapolsky, Professor of biological sciences and neurology at Stanford University (author of *Why Zebras Don't Get Ulcers: A Guide to Stress, Stress-related Disease and Coping*) and by Dr. Bruce Lipton, Ph.D. a cellular biologist and former Fellow at Stanford Medical School.

Think about yourself as being ultimately light energy—for that is what you actually are. The only thing that keeps you here in 3D is breathing. Any form of breathing is a meditation. Using the breath you can alter your awareness. So to meditate allows you to experience the higher or lighter or other aspects of your consciousness that vibrates or resonates at a less dense frequency than the physicality of 3D. To leave 3D you stop meditating in that realm, i.e. you stop breathing. Your consciousness, or the light energy that is you, is then free of its dense physical form (the body) to reconnect with the Soul and through that to return to the Universe and to pass back to it the experience that was learned in 3D. This is how I believe reality works and the reason as to why we are here. We are the experiencing emissaries of a greater power. And we get to play and have fun by creating whatever we want to. Trouble is we got frightened, gave our power away and created hell instead of heaven on earth. Now that you know who you are, you can start to change that now.

The final realization on the path to self knowledge leads you to learn that there is nothing at the end of the road. It is why it is said that it is the journey that matters and not the destination. The destination is merely where the journey has taken you. The experience is the journey. That has been the point of the whole journey. To experience your beliefs. When you stop traveling you have reached your destination and at that point in time you can then see what you have experienced on the journey. It is only the experience that the Soul has that is taken with you from this life. Is God's judgment no more than a greater power examining your experience when you rejoin the Universal energy? There is no good or bad. They are just judgments you have created or someone else's beliefs that you have taken on. So do you really think that your experience will be rejected as not being good enough and you will be denied re-joining your home and sent to hell? No way. There's no such thing as hell anyway—it's just another concept. All experience is valuable and teaches a lesson for the greater good of all.

At the end of the road there is nothing there as such but in that nothing everything becomes apparent. All questions are answered. It is an experience. It can't be described. You'll know it when you get there and when you do your stress will pass and you will believe in the now—no longer in the past or in the future. You will have arrived ready to take the next journey—and that is when the true fun starts. You will have learned that everything is the same and different at the same time. You will see the polarity and understand it. The answers to the mysteries will become obvious. You will trust the process of life, stop resisting it, let go of the struggle and allow the Universe to support you in an elegant and abundant life. You will see the big picture. That is what awaits you. That is the essence of balance, healing and knowing who you are. Life becomes fabulously exciting and full of Love. I am there. It's worth the trip. Believe me.

7.4   LOVE

The Universe is Love energy. Love is the most powerful energy that exists. It heals all. Nothing can withstand its power. It can defeat anything—all disease, imbalance, dysfunction. It fuels the Universe and sustains and nourishes everything in "the Universe". You and I are part of if. We are in our nature made up of Love. When we live in our emotions then we are not in a state of Love but are in our "story". That is a tale that we tell ourselves which we use to separate us from Love and to keep us out of the present moment—the now. It is our emotional states that cause disease. Without Love we get sick and die. That is why it is the subject of so much TV, film, art, theater, literature and poetry. Its what we all seek in our life—some people will even kill for it or kill it when it is denied to them. In the name of Love is one of the oldest defenses and motivations. It is what binds us together as humanity. Everything we do can be traced back to having its origin in wanting Love. We will do anything for it. And I mean anything.

Whenever our hero in literature or film has been faced with choosing between Love and poverty or a material world or career, he has always chosen Love and if he hasn't he has suffered. In the movie *Good Will Hunting*, our hero Will, the one in a million mathematical genius, chooses Love over exposing the secrets of numbers—the Holy Grail of mathematics. Love stories touch us. They make us feel. And for those who do feel this it adds a whole new dimension to life. It makes life rich and colorful and lifts it from the black and white two dimensional nature of thinking and an analytical Mind. We crave Love desperately, if only we were aware of it. You only have to listen to the raw honest lyrics of popular culture. In fact life without Love is so painful that we need to take drugs, have an addiction or create an emotional blockage to manipulate it out of our reality—even if it kills us.

Love is a state of awareness. To experience Love you must be receptive to accessing a state of allowance and acceptance within yourself. Love radiates from your heart and is reflected back to you from your reality so as to feed your Soul and fuel your desire for life and self-expression. Love is an expanding energy unlike Fear that is a contracting energy. It is your birthright to live in a state of Love. Wanting Love lies behind every dream. What you focus on is what you create. So by focusing on Love you will call it towards you. The more Love you have the more you will attract. If you are experiencing conflict in your relationships because you don't accept who or how they are then acceptance will over come this. Noted marriage researcher Andrew Christensen co-author with the late Neil Jacobsen of *Reconcilable Differences* (The Guilford Press) argues that acceptance and not changing the other person is the key to a happier marriage. Acceptance is not about submission. It's about loving your partner because of their differences not in spite of them. You're going to hear a lot more about acceptance in the coming years. It's what was behind the ending of discrimination and equal opportunity employment.

With Love your life becomes peaceful and harmonious. You will not need to control, manipulate, be threatened by Fear nor pain nor need to rely on others for inspiration. Your relationships will be graceful. Understanding the world through metaphysics removes Fear and without Fear you have Love. Love will keep you young at heart and if you feel young you will be young. The most Fearful people age the fastest.

Where judgment is based on the concept of right and wrong it gives an invalid result. There is no such thing as right or wrong. Right and wrong are concepts. Constructs through which to understand the world. They are not truths. They are judgments. If you stopped judging yourself to be right or wrong you would stop punishing yourself. All illness is self punishment.

Trying to be perfect is often used as a way to stop having to judge yourself as being bad. But the search for perfection is a trap. The trap there is that we were taught that if we were perfect then society would reward us and we would receive Love. Sorry. You've been fooled again. And how do you punish yourself when you have failed to live up to your perfect standards or do you rebelliously refuse to be perfect and fail all the time instead? So now is the time to start loving and nurturing yourself instead. That is where the healing will come from. You only think that you are not good enough to be loved. Not being good enough is an emotion, which comes from a judgment of yourself. Many of you believe that you are not deserving of Love. Everyone is deserving of Love. But some people are more willing than others to have it.

Love is the only real link between you and the Universe. Even the emotions are unreal. The Universe is Love. All roads eventually lead there.

The black and white reality of pre 1960 is now gray. You can't count on anything like you used to. The lines are blurring and disappearing. The world is entering a state of chaos and only Love can save you from that. Everything is changing and time is speeding up. Only Love—the energy of life itself—is constant. Without it you can't survive.

The emotional reality is becoming more black and white. Once a little bit of Victim was just that. Imagine that the bathroom of your house is only 5% of your house and that the bathroom for the purposes of analogy is Victimhood. That is, 5% of you is a Victim. When you are in the bathroom all of you is in the bathroom. There is no longer a sense of only being a little bit of a Victim. And when you are there your reality can be created as destructively as if 100% of you was in Victim. Now the consequences are like an avalanche. There are big implications. The emotions are separating. Reality is becoming all or nothing—absolute. Love lets you make the transition from a negative reality to a positive one.

Guilt is the glue that holds your blockages together. Self Pity is the basis of those blockages. Fear is the bottom line in creating all negativity. Love is the glue that holds joy and the Universe together. It's a choice. Your choice.

Love is the only answer to your Ego. You can't out smart or argue with Ego. You bust Ego and use Love to rebuild it. To de-power Ego bring it into the light. If you are not in your true self (that bigger part of who you are which is not acting from a limited aspect of who you are) then you are not coming from Love—it's only adaptive behavior you are demonstrating.

7.41   What Is Love?

Characteristics of the Love energy include being in a state of acceptance (letting things be as they are), compassion (showing sympathy towards your feelings and those of others), forgiveness, healing, intimacy (building close personal relationships), Self Love (valuing and honoring yourself for who you are) and thoughtfulness of yourself and others.

Specifically, Love has certain components.

1. **Giving**: You must be giving of yourself. To sacrifice something. This sacrifice has to be of something you cherish, e.g. your Ego, Victim, control, self importance and the blockages that you pretend are real. You must give to others something that will add to their lives. You need to be doing something nice for them.

2. **Caring**: Caring is a labor to help something grow. Putting yourself out to help someone grow. Sympathy is laziness. There must be no expectation of receiving in return. Its Martyr and Victim, Ego and righteousness if you do. It's not coming from the right place. Caring is its own reward. Caring is a Beingness—it's your nature. The caring is not to please them but to help them grow.

3. **Being Responsible**: You have a different reality if you have Love in your reality. Not just a different perspective on it but a different way of being. This is absolute. Your responsibility is to keep the light of Love on. Love is being able to respond, being willing to respond and actually doing.

4. **Self Acceptance**: This means accepting all aspects of self including the ugly bits too, e.g. your meanness and the other things you find in your Shadow. The Ego has no interest in you accepting yourself. It doesn't want to accept the negative stuff. To change you only have to start accepting the negative stuff because it drops away when you accept it. So release it. Ask the

your Higher Self for forgiveness. Forgive yourself and the negativity goes forever.

5. **Respect:** See those that you Love as they are. Don't see through the judgment of the Ego but in understanding.

6. **Knowing:** You need to know the other person and have awareness of them. There are two ways to know their Soul—

   (i) through pain, e.g. the sadist is never satisfied and will kill but the basis of his pain infliction is his desire to know the other person and

   (ii) through Love by wanting to know their essence.

7. **Humility:** you come to Love with the expectation of newness each time you meet one another. Expecting the same is not humility. You need to have a willingness to see the newness and an acceptance of it. Never taking the object of your Love for granted.

8. **Courage:** This is a willingness to risk the unknown in a reality you create totally. Do it with confidence. You can get hurt that is for sure but if Love is guaranteed without any emotion to it, it's not Love.

Love is the synergy of these 8 components. It's what happens when all eight are present.

Know thyself is the basis of all metaphysics, psychology, religion, sociology, science. To know yourself is the first step back to you.

7.42 Self Love

It is impossible to Love another until such time as you do Love yourself. Religion says, "Love others because Jesus Loves you". Freud sees loving yourself as the start of neurosis and the opposite of loving others. Self Love therefore is the loser's prize because no one else will Love you so you have to Love yourself. The mass consciousness thinking is that you play solitaire and miss out being on the team. But you avoid Self Love to stay with your Ego whose promise is stronger for you. Love of others starts with you loving yourself. It is impossible to Love another until such time as you do Love yourself.

7.43   Why Aren't We Open to Receiving Love?

If you receive Love your reality will go smoothly. If you deny it you are in for many difficulties. The voice within that is calling to receive Love is usually drowned in the Victimhood, rejection, self denial, attempt of the Ego to control, attempts of you to manipulate and the self punishment.

If Love is so fabulous then why aren't we all in Love leading brilliant lives of happiness and joy free of disease?

1. **You think you don't deserve it**. Either because—
    (a)   you are not really that good a person, you are hiding the part of you that is angry, hurt, the punisher, the vindictive nasty person that you are denying, you have a gut feeling of what is in your Shadow, you know all the wrong things you have done, so you self punish or
    (b)   you are not enough yet, e.g. not successful enough, not big enough, not spiritual enough. This is the Ego talking. You are your worst enemy.
2. **You feel Guilty** about receiving Love. You've been taught that its selfish, self centered, Egotistical, unspiritual. Your parents taught you to Love them and to feel Guilty for getting any Love yourself. You were taught to give. You were not taught to receive. The usual suspects also taught you to feel Guilty about receiving Love.
3. Many people see that **receiving Love is a weakness**. You don't need Love if you are successful is the faulty belief. Some people in charities feel strong and better than those they are giving to because they see it as weak to receive and by giving they are in the stronger position.
4. **Fear of obligation**. Teachers, parents, friends imposed conditions on loving you. You now don't want to feel obliged if

someone Loves you. It was a manipulation by them that you bought into because you may not have known better.

5. People sometimes **value their image more than their real selves**, e.g. some people have an image of themselves as always giving while others whose identity is tied to suffering can't let go of that Ego based image. Their Victim/Martyr would be out of a job and they would have to give up their secondary gains of punishing either another person or person or themselves. You get used to the pain of self punishment and even grow to like it thinking that it is Love.

6. Some of us are **too independent** and believe that we can handle everything in our lives ourselves—the Victim and the Martyr would be out of a job if they had nothing to be sorry about—Love would put them out of a job.

7. **The nice guy can't afford to Love**. His behavior is to do things for others. This implies no one does nice things for him. That makes him the nice guy and the others not nice. If he let in Love the person giving to him would be the nice guy and that would make him the not nice guy. His identity is too tied to his behavior to let him change that behavior. He wouldn't know who he was if he received Love. It's his Ego doing it.

8. **You refuse to**—you won't receive it now because you didn't get it long ago when you thought you deserved to get it. You are being childish and petulant at your own expense. Cutting off your nose to spite your face.

9. Many people **see life as a ledger** and think that it is better to be owed than it is to owe.

10. You are **afraid of the responsibility** of receiving Love. If someone chooses to Love you then you don't have to Love him or her back. You think that you do. Receiving Love brings a sense of obligation in the nature of Guilt. But in receiving Love you do have a responsibility to act with integrity, to be honest and to take responsibility for the games and manipulation you may undertake. And you don't think that you can.

11. If you receive Love then **you won't be able to control**, manipulate and punish other people. This is an Ego position for which you get pay offs.

12. Love is the enemy of **the Ego**. If you give into Love then you will have to forego the Ego strokes that you are addicted to or believe to be the truth.

13. People **don't know what Love is**. They only know the pain and hurt they felt as children and have an attitude of who needs it.

7.44   What Are the Pay Offs in Not Receiving Love?

1. You get **not to be responsible**.

2. You get **to punish others**—"no one Loves me anyway" you say "so what does it matter?"

3. You get **to be righteously indignant**.

4. **Self Pity** and its brother self-importance can be played with.

5. You are afraid of Love so you get **to hide behind your Fear of success**, Fear of creativity and Fear of power—Love is success, creativity and being powerful.

7.45   What Are the Effects of Not Receiving Love in Your Life?

1. You will always **struggle**. Love lets in ease and harmony.

2. You **never trust** yourself or your reality. With no Love in your life there is Fear. So because you create your own reality you create situations where you can't trust yourself and you are always afraid of your reality. You create win/lose situations and you are the looser.

3. You begin to **resent and dislike people**—because you live in a Fear based reality you become afraid of everything in it and begin not to trust your reality. You begin to see people as the enemy winning against you. They are the ones you are seeing as not loving you when in fact it is you not letting them in. You magnetically attract people who play out your beliefs.

4.   You always end up **feeling hurt and disillusioned**. Whatever happens you could always have done better or so you think or it could have happened sooner, or it could have been bigger. It's never enough.

5.   You **project parent** onto people. All women become your mother or sister and all men become your father or brother or some other relative. To do this means that you are coming from that place of child within you. In this place you remember all the reasons why you won't receive Love. It keeps those reasons alive. You never get to see who the other person really is. You only see your projection onto them.

6.   You **never feel fully successful**. You may have the trappings of success but you'll never really feel successful. You will always feel that something is missing. You already know that. Once you've achieved your goal there's only momentary satisfaction with it before you have to move onto another goal. These achievements are only symptoms of success. There's no real substance to them. They are illusions. You feel alienated from your reality in a state of Fear and numb to your feelings while all around you is color, sound and abundance.

7.   You **can't give Love**. You don't know how.

7.5   SPIRITUALITY & RELIGION

With all this talk about the Universe it is appropriate to comment on spirituality. The old spirituality meant God and for many people that meant Church and that meant rules about behavior. Would this explain our rebelliousness towards us having a good time even if it kills us—non-acceptance, Guilt, Fear and punishment in hell forever? For Christians especially. Part of my resistance to religion comes from having been raised as a Catholic. All that Fear and Guilt stuff around sex when it was so "wrong" to do it. This is a recipe for disease when viewed from the perspective of the Shadow.

The new spirituality means the study of the Universe. It is the aspect of the unknown within us where all the answers lie. It is about connecting with our source of energy, going into balance and becoming complete.

In other religions and cultures spirituality has always meant a connection with something or someone that is believed to exist even though there is no proof of the existence of that being. A belief that is called faith. Religion and spirituality should not be confused. They are two different things.

As was explained in Chapter 2.1, science and religion used to be the one field of study until they split at the time of the Renaissance. The emergence of vibrational medicine will see them merge again as energy takes us back to the Universe as our source. We are now firmly on the road to proving the existence of the Universe—or what many would call God. The source of the thought energy that keeps us in place through the Etheric Body which by rising resonance goes directly back to it. All energy is connected remember, existing within fields and fields of energy. Quantum is beginning to prove true what metaphysicians have been saying for thousands of years but could not prove. Metaphysics is based on self knowing. Quantum is based on scientific fact. If we are made out of universal energy, which we are, and we are a holographic example of that energy, which we are, then by decoding us could allow for the decoding of the Universe. In other words the decoding of what science calls the Creator or Source of that energy but what religion calls God. In other words science is becoming religion again. The philosophies are beginning to merge and metaphysics is what they have I common.

Religion is adherence to rituals and beliefs that are usually expressed as belonging to an organization, e.g. being of the Catholic religion or the Jewish religion. Spirituality on the other hand is a belief in Spirit, e.g. the North American Indians with their beliefs in the spirit of living beings whether animals or plants, water, earth or air. Deceased ancestors always played a big part. The body might die but the energy that is the spirit always lives on. There was always something that lived on. Some cultures went to extraordinary lengths to accommodate these beliefs—Egyptian, Roman, Greek and Norse mythology especially. Even the Christians believe in a place of Love called Heaven but being religiously (i.e. organizationally) based they also created a place of Fear called Hell (polarity?) as a place of punishment so as to keep us under control. It was that with its eternal punishment for being wrong and the Guilt that we had to carry with it, which caused most of us to forego our spiritual path or connection. We threw the baby out with the bath water. That is changing as the world hungers again for its connection with Divine Energy. Something that will help them make sense of the world and make them feel good about themselves and what they do.

Every culture has a spiritual connection. And the study of and belief in spirituality is now the path of many in the West who are disillusioned with its focus on material success and Ego. In the East where spirituality was freer with its emphasis on philosophy and not on Redemption from sin and it prospered as Buddhism, Hinduism and Shintoism etc. Since Vatican II though the original Christian Church (and the largest Christian Church) has opened its philosophy to universal spiritual liberalism. The planet is now moving globally to merging its divergent spiritual approaches into a global effort. With it is coming a sense of Oneness, co-operation, maturity of consciousness and a movement away from rigid rituals and church laws—in short— personal freedom—unless you are a fundamentalist Christian that is.

In learning about metaphysics it is completely unavoidable not to come across spirituality. All roads lead to Rome so they say and the further you go along the road from what is very much our day to day life and take it back to the Universe you will end up at spirituality. It is inevitable.

7.6   CONCLUSION

In evolving, the human consciousness developed an Ego as a means to gather information from the world around it. The Ego was over-worked, went bad and set out on a path of misinformation and became a life threat to its host—you. Lost in that evolution were the child and the adolescent aspects of who you are and these were caught up in an emotional prison which impacted on the human in the now. These energies need to be freed for the human to continue to evolve as a consciousness. Any energy that wasn't expressed or felt in the human's development was harbored by the human in its Shadow. This too impacts on the human in the now relieving it of its freedom to think without influence from unresolved and denied internal conflicts. Those feelings need to be accepted and released to enable evolution to continue. Now free of impediment the human is able to re-connect with the higher aspects of its consciousness so as to be the true master of its domain. Free of the energies that controlled its Mind it is ready to create its own world. To create it's own reality using thought, attitudes and choices.

In coming into the density of 3D you forgot that you were con-nected to a greater source of energy. It is now time for you to put aside the pride of Ego and to ask for help from those parts of yourself that you have until now not been aware of. It is the Ego that says that you have to do it all alone. That is a trap. Listen to me. That is a trap. Learn how to ask for help. Learn to ask for aid. The purpose of the Inner World is to help you get as much experience as possible. Your Higher Self is connected to the Universe—God. Use that connection to make your life elegant and free from the struggle and hardship that the Ego has led you to believe is the only way to success. Your Ego has led you into imbalance, disease and for some of you the prospect of death. If that is what you want then fine, but if you are reading this book now then there is a good chance that you want to live, and let me tell you, when you do come into balance and access your universal power then you will live like you have never lived before. You will never be alone again. You will always have Love in your life and you will feel satisfied and content and you will have a better life. Instead of seeking the fruits of your labors they will come to you and people will marvel at your success. It is worth giving up the old way of the Ego and facing the Fear and then pushing through it discovering the beautiful person you always were. You just couldn't see it through the dirt that you had collected on the journey. It is time now to clean up your act. The choice is yours. There is so much Love and help waiting for you in the Inner World—Love that you can feel. Help that is real.

SO WHO ARE YOU THEN? Your Ego is only an interface between the outside world you experience with your five senses and the internal world of the essence of who you are. A careful analysis will reveal that you are none of these things. The fact is there is no "you" as such. So who then is doing the thinking? Clearly the Universe is. It uses you as its instrument for playing out the concepts of the Universal Mind. So you are in the Universe and the Universe is in you and all reality is occurring in the consciousness of the Universe. On that level then—within universal consciousness—your life and everything in it is real. On our level of consciousness it remains an illusion—a hologram of light held together by thought energy—and for that reason it can be changed with the light of the Universe as quickly as you can manage it. Isn't a quick change also called a miracle? And where do they come from? Anything now becomes possible. You don't have to work out how it will happen—the Universe will re-arrange the molecules—just see yourself where you want to be. It's all about intention.

But what's the point then you ask if you don't do anything and the Universe is doing it all? Am I not creating my own reality? Yes you are. You get to make the choices. The variables of your Negative Ego, your denial and Shadow, the lack of Love in your life, your energy bodies together combine to produce the unpredictable and so do you. This is a Planet of free will. But it is your humility in recognition of a greater power that will finally bring you away from the pain that these variables produce in your life, so that one day you will allow the Love of the Universe to flow through you so that you too will have everything that the Universe always intended you to have— peace, Love, contentment, happiness and abundance. It's your choice.

DIVISION III

—MAKING THE NEW YOU AND YOUR NEW LIFE: BRINGING YOUR ENERGY INTO ALIGNMENT

Chapter 8

—An Integrated Approach To Healing

8.1   INTRODUCTION

The biggest thing to remember is that it is human to be ill. There isn't one of us who has never been ill. All illness comes from Fear and lack of Love. It is the mental aspects that cause these emotional blockages and dysfunction. Sometimes they cause us to eat things that physically cause illness or modification of our DNA thus creating problems for our off spring. Therefore any changes we make to our Energy System have to be seen as a healing. Holistic healing is all about healing everything so this Chapter starts talking about the nature of healing. Even if you are not ill—you will be eventually and prevention is better than cure—you should read this chapter.

Even if you don't think that you have blockages in your chakras, Etheric, Emotional or Mental Bodies you should read those chapters. Denial is a subtle and powerful intruder. You can be easily convinced that there is nothing wrong with you. If you have ever been ill then there is something out of alignment. If you can guarantee yourself that you will never be ill again then stop reading now. I can guarantee that almost all of you have blockages in all your energy bodies. 99% of you for sure. Illness is the result of blockages. Before illness manifests these disturbances show up as problems in your life—crime, failure, lack of money, food, good times, Love, friends. If neglected these problems turn into diseases within you as well as you still having all those outside problems. You need to see Division III as a healing chapter. Heal yourself and let the Love in so that you can have freedom, success, abundance, Love and friends. It's why you're reading this book anyway. Don't stop now. It is at this point that your Ego is fighting its strongest to have you not finish this book. It's putting up all sorts of reasons—all sorts of reasons. Anything you feel now is coming from your Ego. It knows that it will loose it position of superiority and that you will take back your power. It is too stupid to know and too fat on Fear and negativity to realize, that if you do take back your power, it can rest and stop having to be right all the time and stop having to prove it's the best or the worst all the time. You will in fact be doing your Ego a huge favor in returning it to its divinely created role.

You see, if you didn't want your life to be better then you would never have read this far. There must be some blockage somewhere that is stopping you from having a better life—even if that blockage is lack of information—otherwise you wouldn't be reading this book. If you want to have a better life then somewhere within you Love is unable to reach you here on Earth.

This Division III will give you many techniques so that you can put your energy bodies into alignment. I have seen and done many techniques over the past 18 years in an attempt to investigate and to create new beliefs. But the most beneficial and simplest has been the techniques of Byron Catie. She is at www.thework.org. I have used her technique on myself and on other people and it works incredibly well. It takes you out of the story and shows you your beliefs. It makes you own that which you are creating. It removes the smoke screens that you have so cleverly set up for yourself.

Our bodies break down daily—always being rebuilt but never quite to the level that they had been in the previous cellular pattern. Our cells duplicate but the copies are never being quite as good as the originals from which they came. Like a photocopy of a photocopy of a photocopy of a photocopy, eventually the picture fades away as so many old people do. Interesting analogy too—photo meaning light—given that we are made of light. On one level our bodies are advanced photocopying machines. Antioxidants help overcome the problem of the cellular dysfunction by attacking the free radicals that are responsible for the breakdown. Free radicals are the pollutant by-product of us breathing—the very thing that keeps us here. In other words there is an in-built self destructive mechanism that ensures that we eventually return to the place from which we came. Man has always wanted to play God. Science has been his tool. Science comes up with ways to prolong life. Hence the reverence to science. Medicines tend to cure symptoms but not the causes of them so that the symptoms emerge else where later as different symptoms or as the same symptoms all over again—the endless runny nose is a good example. Allergies is another. Not that there's anything wrong with treating symptoms so long as medicine isn't trying to pass itself off as actually healing someone. Only you can heal yourself. And you can use medicine to help you in the management of that process. But you need to use all the medicines available and treat the machine top to bottom. If the body is out of whack then one or more of your energy bodies must be as well. Because that is where the original dysfunction came from.

If our cells are breaking down on a physical level then ultimately and logically the cure would be to re-educate the mass consciousness and have it believe on a cellular level that respiration doesn't cause cell dysfunction. That would be a help. One person working alone has the power to do that to themselves anyway. We create our own DNA. But such levels of evolutionary consciousness are far off. In the 1998 science fiction film *Dark City*, the beings all thought the same thoughts at the same time and in that way re-created the city each night. It's the same theme.

So on one level each of us is ill—it's a gradual thing called aging. During this process of maturation that we call "life" we all have experiences of what it is like to be alive. Life is not just about functioning from day to day—eating, sleeping, working, having sex, socializing, moving from place to place—on a deeper level it is all about being and feeling alive. As each of us gets older we begin to realize this. Most of us realize that it is quality of life that matters. Not quantity in life. The exceptions are those in poverty and of course you can never have too much Love.

We are therefore not only diseased from aging daily, but some of us have physical disease that doctors have been able to label. All pain is symptomatic of disease. Whether it is physical or emotional pain. It's your body telling you that something is not in balance.

If life is all about expanding and growing (are we any different in that regard to the birds and trees?) then if we are not expanding and reaching up into the light but being stagnant, stunted and in the pain of darkness, then we are diseased. You can grow through pain—there is no mistake about that. But if you had the choice—wouldn't you prefer to grow though happiness and peace? It's so much easier. Believe me. It really is.

Growing out of Fear and its offspring, pain has hindered our development. The rest of us who aren't in our own eyes successful, who have not reached our full potential, who are afraid to do what we want to (even though we know that to do so would make us happy) and especially for those who are not at peace or happy, then we too are diseased or unrealized. Our way of thinking and feeling is out of balance.

From a simplistic metaphysical point of view the causes of all disease can be found by looking at the reality that the person is coming from. Each disease has its own characteristic and while the factual circumstances leading up to discovery of the symptoms may differ from person to person, once you can recognize the pattern the actual energetic causes of the disease are easily identified in the person's life. Doctors have often thought about the mind-body connection in looking for the cause of disease. In fact the present trend is for patients to take an active part in their own healing. The "patient" is no longer still and inert.

Metaphysics provides the missing link in this study and lets the healer see where the disease has its cause. He or she is therefore able to know where to start in his healing. I'll say it again. It is that important. The healer is always the ill person. The ultimate healer is you. Say it again to yourself now. This is the first lesson of healing. If you expect your doctor or your drugs to do it for you and to just sit back and not change anything in your life then very few of you will survive a serious illness and the rest of you will eventually contract a serious illness. It is inevitable, unless you change. Belief creates reality. If your reality is diseased your beliefs are faulty (i.e. Fear based) and you need to create new beliefs. Talk to yourself about this. It is the inner dialogue that is the important one. Nothing else is real. Everything on the outside of you is an illusion—a projection of beliefs. It's only good for getting clues and having experiences. And it is more fun when you are not buying into a painful reality created by Fear. It's your choice. No one is going to do it for you and the sooner you take responsibility for that and therefore your life the sooner you are going to see an improvement in you, your life and you in your life. It is called taking back your power from the images that you see on the outside of you. You see them out there and think that they are real and treat them as if they are. They are just playing back to you, like a teasing temptress who never delivers. That is your Ego and its addiction to the illusion. Most people are addicted to what they see. This is really important to understand. They believe their own publicity. Why wouldn't they? It is real to them. They are hooked on living in this outside world of desire, which has been built on Fear and the need to keep Fear alive. The pity of it all. They are not to be blamed. They know no better. Until now. The secret is out. You can do whatever you want to. Take back your power. Then work with someone who can help you. But it always comes back to you. This is not something to be afraid of. In fact it is something that will free you forever into being the powerful and confident person that you really are underneath all that Ego and projection.

If you can identify the area of stress that is making you lose energy, then if you can fix it before it turns into a physical problem, then you should not get ill. All stress comes from either the past or more usually the future. It is anticipation of what might be that frightens you.

Because you live in a Fear based reality you expect fearful things to happen to you that will frighten you. All of them relate to threats to your safety. Where to start with examples? There are so many of them—just read the front page of a Murdoch owned newspaper or listen to Fox News and you'll get the idea—you will be told that it is not safe in the world.

Some prime examples are—

1. **Shortages**. The Y2K bug was a great creation for the people most afraid—they really loved getting anxious about that—some even built fortresses and armed themselves for the end of the world—very exciting stuff;

2. **Pollution**. In every aspect of our lives—water, food, air, visual, land, in space, ideas;

3. **Crime**. The more violent and repugnant the better. This is my favorite—you get to lock yourself away in your own home, you watch it on TV, Larry King interviews Victims of it—get a clue everyone—"Victims" says it all—no more Victims would mean no more crime on the planet!;

4. **Violence**. Can I say to you—The Terminator, Freddie Kruger, the horror movie genre (life isn't scary enough for these people they need to be entertained by it by seeing other people's live more scary lives than their own). On one level though it is a way for people for face their Fears as stored in the Shadow. On another it just gives people violent ideas. School children kill school children. They have learned from TV that it is OK to use guns to settle a problem. I see people being shot at 11am on Saturday morning TV and wonder why more school children haven't already died. You really have to wonder what is in the Minds of TV programmers who play this sort of material at times when children have full access to TV. We have no one to blame but ourselves for the world in which we live.

5. **Loosing something**. Like your spouse, partner, job, money or your health. As if any of those needs any explaining. The joy of the stock market ride perpetuates Fear. The risks we take to

win gives us a rush and winning is often just a cheap hit of power especially if we have manipulated or lied or struggled to win.

Uncertainty is the key to Fear. Therefore Fear produces the need to control. And that is what the law does because we as a people no longer can trust ourselves to enforce our own laws. From Fear comes greed. From greed comes a belief in shortages and limitation. Again the law steps in. It is a mechanism that we have created to protect ourselves from ourselves. If everyone was in integrity and there was no Fear then there would be no lawyers. Imagine a world without police, lawyers and judges. How much television is devoted to those jobs now? And I don't just mean the soaps. How much simpler would your life be if you knew that you would never again encounter the law? What a relief that would be. If people were freed from Fear—then that reality is a possibility. And if everyone could heal himself or herself there'd be no doctors. What? No law and no medicine? Half the drama on TV would disappear. Get it—dramas. That is what life has become. A drama. Do you need drama in your life to feel alive? Apparently so if your level of feeling is so numbed that you have to watch it on TV at night. You are hooked on Fear. But can you begin to see what sort of a new world could be created. Here in America the crime rate is falling and has been for some time. Officials are saying that it is related to prosperity having increased. I believe that part of the credit goes to those people who have lifted themselves out of Fear. America is renowned in the world for having led the New Age and the fruits of this drive towards to self discovery and responsibility are beginning to be seen.

And while I am talking about a whole new world let's just quickly mention the drug scene and its role in crime. If the addicts didn't need to numb out to their feelings then they wouldn't need to take their drugs. Remove Fear and people would want to feel their realities because they would be realities of Love. Can you see how many resources would be freed up?

And the defense forces wouldn't be required either. That would free up unbelievable amounts of money that could be applied towards to education, the arts, early retirement. People have too much of a vision of war in space—they are spreading the disease of this planet into space. That has to stop. It can only attract war to this planet. What you put out you get back.

To identify the area of your stress you need to know who you are so that you can be in touch with your intuition. Finding out who you are is called waking up. So waking up is the first step on the path of rewards that being aware offers you. Division III is all about waking up by getting in touch with who you are.

Personal power is necessary for health. In **The Road Less Traveled** M Scott Peck said that seeing and admitting the truth about ourselves, about our role in creating our own problems, and how we relate to others is vital for healing. Dr. John Harrison says the same thing in his best seller **Love Your Disease**. Our attitudes and belief patterns are indications of how we use power. Everything we do in life involves power issues—controlling others or being controlled by them, feelings of powerfulness or inadequacy. People make things mean power to them—money, career, the right address, owning their own home, the labels on their clothes and jewelry and/or an attractive or rich or famous partner in life. So if they lose one or more of these things then their health suffers because they have lost their outside validation— the thing to which they have given their power. Power is the ability to act. It means nothing more than that. Knowledge is power. And as I have already said, knowledge is light—male energy. And we are made of light. We are therefore already powerful. We have just denied it through Fear of our very own potential. Nelson Mandela said this too. It is the thing we Fear the most. Our own power. So why would we give away our power when we need it to run our lives? No wonder we get drained by life. No power=no energy=the machine that is the physical body rusting out and running down=aging which leads to disease and death.

We give away our power in return for approval from others. This is how we get our Love. If others approve of us then we must be good enough to be loved. As I said before—the thing that every single person on this Planet wants is Love. It is instinctive it is so much a part of what we are. It is why winning is associated with Love. And perfection too. One leads to the other. Love stops us from being separate. Separateness causes pain. We separate ourselves from others through the contemptuous judgments of the Ego, which feeds on Fear.

Our choices are expressions of our personal power. Sometimes we agree to do things that are asked of us because we believe that the other person has more power than we do. What you are actually doing is judging yourself as being less than they are. You need to become conscious of what gives you power and your relationship to them. This will hasten you becoming whole.

Everyone can become whole. All disease is therefore healable. We just have to encourage people to take back their power and make a decision to really want to be whole.

Are you going to continue to support the belief of the mass consciousness and perhaps the belief that you feel that you do not deserve to be whole and that disease is some sort of inevitable outcome of living? Or do you choose to be open to the view that in spite of the massive odds that conspire against you that somehow it is possible not only to lead a normal life (whatever that is to you) but in fact to escape from disease all together? Because you can. Even if it is only 1% of your consciousness that wants to do it. You can. That 1% can become 2%. That 2% can become 4% and before you know it, little by little, then in bigger jumps, you are moving towards 50%. With the momentum of the success behind you and the vision at the end of the tunnel in front of you, wholeness becomes a probable reality for you. Once the momentum starts you'll look back and wonder why you did not do it sooner.

Do you see the job ahead as being a mammoth rock to crack? A rock that can't be side stepped and which is too big to be climbed? If you do then you probably also see a glass that has 50% of its volume as being half empty. Others with optimism see it as being half full. Chip away at your rock until it is only a pile of stones that you can skip over. And every time you walk over them it will become easier and easier to do.

I know that it is easier to go with the powerlessness and the resultant inertia of staying where you are in your life than it is to stop yourself in your tracks and take back your power by saying, "in spite of what I believe, I can become whole and I will become whole, I can change and I will change." This takes courage and strength. You do not have to believe you can do it. At this time it only has to be your intention that you want to. Go down into your feelings now and feel that pain and despair and Fear and doubt. This is what is keeping you stuck where you are now. So now draw on the energy of those feelings (it doesn't matter what emotions, energy or feelings that you are using if you are only using them for the purpose of fueling your intention—it's all just energy driving the thought) and feeling the words say "in spite of what I believe, I can become whole and I will become whole, I can change and I will change."

By acting "as if" the changes have occurred will be enough to give your body the message that a change has been made. As you begin to see the changes yourself, the inertia will shift in response to the new power that you see yourself exercising and your new beliefs about healing and becoming whole will become conscious.

Cellular memory holds our experiences. For disease to occur Carolyn Myss says that negative emotions have to be dominant, and what accelerates the process is knowing the negative thought to be toxic and giving it permission to thrive in your consciousness anyway, e.g. remaining obsessively angry makes you more likely to develop a disease because the energy consequence of negative obsession is powerlessness. Energy is power, and transmitting energy into the past by dwelling on painful events drains power from your present day body and can lead to illness. In other words stay in the moment—the now. Whenever your Mind takes you to the past you re-create the past.

8.2   WHAT IS DISEASE?

The word disease is a combination of "dis" meaning the opposite of and "ease" meaning freedom from pain and struggle. So disease means "being in pain or struggle". Many people think of disease as being a terminal condition, an illness needing hospitalization, a condition requiring treatment by a doctor or with self-administered medication. It is these things. But it is also an unhappy life, failure and having unexpressed feelings. So on one level just about everyone is in a state of disease.

To be in a state of disease means that your energy is out of balance. Out of harmony. This usually manifests in the Outer World as physical illness as described in the previous paragraph or as things going "wrong" in your life or you not being successful when trying to create something in your life. All of these things cause pain. In your search to learn who you are, you will see that you are diseased. The person you think you are is not well either at the level of the Etheric Body, Emotional Body, Mental Body or Causal Body. This unwellness is caused by an energy blockage at one or more of these levels. Therefore the person you see in front of the mirror is not the person you would see if you had no energy blockages. The person without blockages would be in harmony and everything in their life would be working as they wanted it to—and it would be a harmonious person who was doing the choosing, not a diseased person who must by definition therefore be creating a diseased reality. You see, if your energy is out of balance then your reality s out of balance. Sick people create sick lives. Well people create well lives. Successful people create successful lives and those who think of themselves as second best come second. The successful life doesn't create the successful person. The person with the successful life was already successful. That's the difference. You have to be well first and if you are not then no amount of trying to fix it on the outside will work permanently. The old pattern will repeat itself. Worse than that, your continual failure will reinforce your lack of confidence and this will contribute to your sense of not being good enough and that in turn will lead to sabotage. So it becomes an endless downward spiral that sees you eventually totally numbed out to the pain with all sorts of addictions or just stagnant and slipping towards complete inertia.

In knowing who you are—because you can't see who you are until you see the whole of you—you not only have to be able to identify the parts that make you up, but you have to be able to identify when those parts are out of alignment and know what to do to bring them into alignment. Only then will you know who you are. And we have established that you are out of alignment. So can you begin to see why this Division of the book deals with bringing you back into alignment and why you need to be?

So for the rest of this Division I will talk about healing. Healing means to bring back into alignment, harmony and balance.

By integrating different techniques (called "modalities") simultaneously, there is a synergistic benefit. That is, a benefit that is greater than the sum of the parts, e.g. 1+1=4. All of us are different. What works for one person does not work as well for another. The benefit of integrated medicine (i.e. using more than one technique at the same time to treat different levels of our Energy System) is that there is no right or wrong way to heal yourself. There are only options you choose to suit yourself in your healing. You may choose acupuncture, diet, yoga and Gestalt. Another person may choose Tai Chi, homeopathy, Radionics and Ayuervedic Medicine.

Metaphysics underscores all modalities. It is the philosophical framework through which to understand how healing and disease occur. Fortunately for me I put my faith in metaphysics and through that learning experience shifted away from disease to a life where I pretty well get everything I want. I am not perfect and am learning all the time but the corner has been well and truly turned and I am well on the way down the path to being completely balanced and whole. Almost no negativity impacts on my life. It is often a series of magical coincidences .

Most people will not take responsibility for their own lives so they loose themselves in their outside world through work, relationships, addictive behavior, being pre-occupied, drama, staying busy (almost obsessively so) or by numbing out, e.g. getting stoned, getting plastered, partying all night and day to the extent that it is almost an art form, taking substances to make them feel good and to forget, obsessively working at looking good and the list goes on. It's all diversion and procrastination (i.e. self punishment) and this is not the way that a healthy adult lives.

Energy was not meant to be held onto but allowed to flow. You are like a sieve through which energy passes. Light entering and leaving as it does through your chakras. Imagine that sieve with a blockage. You would become like a balloon swelling up with energy as it is stopped from passing through. The energy that is built up eventually slows down until it is resonating as form, i.e. as part of your physical body. In doing so it interrupts the functioning of your physical body. This is what physical disease is, e.g. cancer. Or it starts to distort your projections into the world so that they are not manifesting as you intended them to be. I'll use the example of the Anger blockage again. In this case, everything in your life is tinged with Anger, e.g. frustrating delays, snipes and sarcasm from people, road rage from other people, telephone operators hanging up on you, your cell phone going dead at the wrong time, people cutting in front of you inline at the supermarket or being delayed at checkout because of a fight they are having with the cashier, you witnessing a mugging or you experiencing discrimination.

Health and illness refer to states of being. Love is a state of being. In the state of Love there is no room for anything else.

A body can't do anything by itself. It has no power to do so. A corpse can't move. A body is only alive when it has consciousness. Let's use the analogy of a radio—the body is a radio, consciousness is the electricity (energy source without which the body would be silent) and the source of the information that is broadcast. Your Ego is the announcer. When the body is "in tune" and all aspects of it are working properly then there is harmony. When the needle is not on the station there is static and the message is lost. The out of tuneness is illness. The body is the instrument of consciousness. Not the other way around.

Your body is an instrument that tells you when something is wrong in the messages that you are receiving. I will use a car as an example. The car is your body. Traveling along through life a warning light comes on in the dashboard (you notice a pain somewhere). The light indicates that something is wrong. What do you do? Ignore it until the brake fluid has drained out and you end up rear ending the person in front of you and then you blame the car manufacturer for faulty brakes (i.e. you play Victim) or do you heed the warning, take responsibility and have the car checked and rectify the problem? Your symptoms— whether physical or out there in the world—are telling you that something is wrong, e.g. your boyfriends keeps standing you up on dates. Hello. Get a clue. You are the constant in the equation. What is wrong with your thoughts for this to keep happening?

Traditional medicine would disengage the warning light, i.e. remove the symptom, e.g. surgery or pain killers. You know that you can't deny the symptoms forever and that eventually if you do then you will die as the symptoms get worse and worse. Eventually you will be killed in the car accident because the failed brakes and let the car drive over the cliff.

The symptom is saying that we are sick on an energy level. It is the first sign that the energy is starting to go wrong. We get so used to things going wrong in our life that we ignore them or treat them as being normal then preach that as being normal to our peers, children, parents, school teachers and governments. This "wrongness" is then perpetuated as "this is life". Life doesn't have to be like this. Life is what you make it to be. There's a great line in Bette Midler's movie *Drowning Mona* when greasy spoon diner waitress Jamie Lee Curtis says, "luck doesn't happen to people like us. Luck happens to Madonna." Madonna wouldn't agree. She made her life happen and she will be the first to tell you that in the beginning when she went against the grain of her old beliefs that life was a struggle. But as her beliefs changed and the momentum of her success compounded she became one of the most influential people of the late 20th Century.

To be whole and free of symptoms is to be re-connected to consciousness without blockage. It is to know yourself. It is also called enlightenment. This is the goal of the person seeking spiritual mastery. I believe that one of the purposes that we have here on earth is to become enlightened—to realize who we are. This is a step that we could be ready to take here now. This is the next step in evolutionary consciousness. Once taken we as a humanity will enter the long prohesized "Golden Age"—a 1,000 years of peace—that will arrive with the advent of the Age of Acquarius. We are on the verge of this period. Astrologically the Age has begun. As we move further away from the Age of Pisces the age of peace will become more and more of a reality. There may be a few fading storms of Anger, war and struggle as we move further away from it but I believe that conscious enlightenment on the planet is inevitable. The signs are there now.

Enlightenment also means getting well. The more we heal, the stronger our connection to the Universe becomes and the more we know who we are. Traditional medicine comes from the point of view that we are basically healthy and can be "protected from illness". If that is so then why are so many people still sick—physically and emotionally and in their living? Medicine keeps getting better at what it does—we all are living longer—but we keep getting ill and new diseases keep happening while old ones becomes resilient to treatments such as penicillin. And we become more ill as we age. So much so that we accept it as being normal. I know that genetic engineering holds hope for the future but that may not be totally successful unless we change the beliefs that underwrite the DNA. DNA is a data record of mass conscious beliefs. We can change our own DNA. Our beliefs about old age are stored here so successfully that we will break down physically when we age and get ill and die. But DNA is the beginning and the end of the scientific breakthrough and completing the Gnome Project (the de-coding of DNA) won't change the world. DNA is only part of the scheme of things. Cellular structure is the result of the energy fields that caused it to be. One day science will step back even further to find this. Even now the technology has not been created to read the DNA that has been uncovered and it is thought that it may be decades before it is.

8.3   WHAT IS HEALING?

I have mentioned this before. But to wrap up the introduction to this Division I will briefly go through it again in essence and in detail. Let me talk in more detail about healing and being cured and give you another example.

If you only deal with the symptom, the underlying cause will continue to manifest the disease, e.g. you can keep getting rid of the boy friends after they stand you up but until you look at the reason why they do this then you will keep having boy friends who stand you up.

Another example, in May 1998 in the Sydney newspaper *the Sun Herald* I read about a woman who was taking a new drug for breast cancer. This woman's symptoms left her but then she contracted uterine cancer (another female sex organ). As the disease could not manifest in one form it moved to another area where it tried again to give the person a message. Removing the warning light from the dashboard won't stop you one day from having a car accident. Because of this experience this person is now putting into the Minds of other woman that this drug causes uterine cancer. Other woman who have been using the drug could now expect to manifest uterine cancer too—if they choose to believe it or if they were in denial of their disease.

Curing a patient previously meant the patient sitting there while the cure was administered to them. In the New World of independence a healing occurs when the patient is active—active in seeking out the truth. The truth really will set you free. You examine new options and means. You expand your Mind. You actively heal all aspects of who you are. You look at the choices and attitudes you have made in life and see how these have contributed to who you are. It involves self examination and self awareness. You acquire the will to use your energy for the creation of Love, Self Esteem and health. When you choose to heal an energy connection occurs as you embrace the therapy. Self healing is to co-operate with the natural healing tendency that is built into you.

A healing arises from the notion that the body is a multi-dimensional entity. It applies to the whole body. A healing is a journey. An education as to who you are. It is part of making yourself a better and stronger person.

Today healing is undergoing a paradigm shift, i.e. one thought model is entirely being replaced by a completely separate, distinct and unrelated thought model. Not only are we becoming aware of accepting everything so as to end conflict and polarity—both internal and external, we are discovering the physics of the universe, the metaphysics and the quantum physics and the opening to new healing models. We are discovering the healing power of light—the essence of what we are made.

Art is said to imitate life and story telling uses the medium of the time to express it. Story telling has gone from charcoal on cave walls and sitting by the nightly camp fire to Rembrandt, opera and theater to moving pictures stored on film. From that we went very quickly to magnetic tape and now to the digital universe—VCD and DVD as light randomly (no longer in linear analog) stored on metal. Sound has gone from being stored as ink markings on paper, to wax, then vinyl through a paradigm shift to magnetic tape (the cassette) to light randomly (no longer in linear analog) stored on metal. Even power generation has gone from fossil fuel to nuclear to solar. Medicine is and will more and more move from the Newton to the Einstein Model—from a flesh and bone machine to a hologram made of light held together by thought energy. Of the late 20th Century it will be said that pure light was discovered as a source of energy that could be harnessed as technology. We are starting to use what we are made up of so it makes sense that light will heal light. That thought will heal. Re-tuning and raising resonance is the new way.

8.4   INTERPRETING YOUR OWN SYMPTOMS

As long as people look for causes then they will find them. This is an absolute truth. These causes are the product of their own expectation. Ultimately though how far back you go is up to you in looking for the cause of the cause of the cause. What causes the cause that caused the cause? You have to stop at some point and say that this was the thing, event or person, which caused the cause in question.

The past and the future determine everything. Illness, disease, disharmony, imbalance—it's all the same. A symptom merely uses what is available to it as a means of communicating the underlying energy in a tangible form—it's trying to say something to you.

The Shadow will demonstrate itself through disease. One cause of disease is denial. Looking in the past for causes is us blaming a "cause" for what we have. Instead we should be taking responsibility for ourselves and looking at the message that the disease is trying to tell us. We create the meaning anyway so why not create it and then deal with it accordingly.

Bacteria do not cause disease. We use it as a tool for manifesting illness. Paint does not cause a picture on a canvas. We use it as a tool to bring the picture into being. Why does bacteria infect some people and not others? It's what our energy attracts to ourselves that matters.

So in trying to understand your symptoms ignore all causes of them. The causes are merely the means of manifestation of the disease.

Work out exactly the point in time when the symptoms appeared. Look at what was happening in your life at the time, your thoughts then, fantasies, dreams, events and how items of news went into making up the symptoms' framework.

The language of the symptoms will give you a clue as to what is wrong.

Almost all symptoms make us change. They stop us doing what we would like to do and they make us do what we never intended to do. We should let our disturbances disturb us. A symptom corrects imbalances. The symptom forces into the open the polarity that we have been denying. Pay more attention to it. The question becomes: "what is the symptom stopping me from doing and what is the symptom making me do generally?" This will lead you to the area of the illness' central theme.

Extremism generally means that there is a problem. The shy one and the show off both lack self confidence. Our Unconsciousness remains unwhole until we have actually succeeded in integrating the Shadow. In the act of experiencing the symptom we go into consciousness because it is only in the psyche that learning, perceiving and experiencing occur. So problems provide us with an opportunity for learning. Our problems escalate from gentle provocation to severe pressure. The more we resist the more pressure that the symptoms will put on us.

The scale of severity in symptoms manifesting to us is as follows

a.   thoughts, wishes, fantasies
b.   functional disturbances, e.g. aches
c.   more acute physical disturbances, e.g. inflammations, wounds, minor accidents
d.   chronic conditions, e.g. heart attack
e.   incurable diseases, e.g. cancer
f.   death either through illness, accident or Victimhood
g.   congenital deformity through karma.

Before a symptom shows up in the body it shows up in the Mind. If you are open to your conscious impulses, the more you are prepared to give them free reign, the more unorthodox and lively you life will be. This is where imagination comes from and this explains why creative people (especially younger less constrained creative people) tend to be unconventional.

If we are fixed and rigid we deny these impulses and this makes us unreceptive to our psychological side. Psychological impulses need to be lived out because if they aren't then they will manifest as symptoms. In the beginning these inflammations arise as an "-itis", e.g. conjunctivitis. As they get worse they become an "-osis", e.g. thrombosis. Eventually they become incurable and you die. Whatever was not dealt with at death comes back with us as karma in the next life. So while we come into this life with a new body we do so with an old consciousness.

As we get older we become more of our Ego and get further away from our Unconscious, i.e. we get stuck, so we become more prone to disease symptoms.

Chapter 9

—USING THE ENERGY OF THE ETHERIC BODY

9.1 CHAKRA ALIGNMENT —CHROMOTHERAPY

If we are made from light and part of our body is ill (i.e. one or more of our energy bodies is discordant) then if we are bombarded with light that is at the frequency of wellness then the discordant resonance is lifted by the input of the new energy to its proper level—this then restores or heals. This is the theory behind all vibrational medicine—the medicine of the 21st century. Why do gray skies lead to depression? Why do you feel better after a day at the beach in the sunshine? Chromotherapy is the answer—healing with colored light. In the mid 1980's I saw a great little book called *Color Meditations* and these addressed these issues as well as providing lots of meditations that you can do with color.

First you diagnose the problem by its symptoms or where it is manifesting in the body or the emotions. It will help to refer to the table in Chapter 4.3. This will let you identify the chakra that is being affected and whether it is the Emotional, Mental or Causal Body from which the blockage is coming from. The following diet table will show what food corresponds to which chakra. This is the first stage in balancing. The next step is to go to the next energy level—the Emotional Body.

COLOR	FUNCTION	FOOD
Red = life, strength, vitality	Stimulates and warms	Beets, radishes, plums, spinach, currants, black cherries
Orange = energy	Absorbs and stimulates vital energy, affects digestion and assimilation and visualization of ideas, antidote to repression and limitations, induces self confidence and positive thinking, fosters optimism, courage and the will to succeed	Oranges, apricots, mangoes, peaches, cantaloupe, carrots
Yellow = mind and intellect	Aids in the creation of thought and in visualization, arouses optimism, cheerfulness and a balanced outlook on life	Lemons, bananas, corn, pineapple, grapefruit
Green = harmony and sympathy	Nervous well being, proper bodily functioning, energy of the sun in its safest & most natural form	All green vegetables and fruits
Blue = inspiration & devotion	Features true peace, poise, harmony, serenity and raises consciousness to the realm of spirit	Grapes, black berries, blue plums, all blue fruit and vegetables
Indigo = mystic borderland	An antidote to frustrations, the Fear complex, general negative conditions, extends inner vision, opens new fields of comprehension and knowledge	All foods used for blue and violet
Violet = spirituality	Aids the development of spiritual consciousness. Clairvoyance, psychic sensitivity, valuable in meditation and concentration exercises, inspires the mind, arouses Soul qualities, mysticism, spiritual intuition, idealism	Eggplant, blackberries, grapes, beets

9.2   CHAKRA ALIGNMENT—LOOKING AT THE ISSUES

Caroline Myss approaches the subject by looking at the issues that each chakra represents. Align and heal the energy represented by the issues and you realign the chakras. This is the opposite approach to Chromotherapy but there is no reason why both approaches can't be used.

The purpose in her approach is self analysis. It is an approach based on Chapter 2 where the question is asked—"what beliefs must I have in order to have the experience that I am having?" If you want to know this then at the end of each chapter of her book has many of the questions that you would want to ask. Understanding that work will be a big step towards you finding out who you are. I thoroughly recommend her book on work in the chakra area.

9.3   YOGA

While yoga is a practice and is part of the Hindu tradition of healing, which comes under the heading of Ayuervedic Medicine (see Chapter 13.10), it works to unblock energy in the body.

Primarily it was developed to prepare the student for prayer and spiritual enlightenment. Today in the West it is more used as a stress reduction technique. The practice involves stretching and breathing exercises. This loosening lets the blocked energy to escape. As the energy is released a feeling of relaxation and well being permeates the Energy System. The chakras open and clear allowing the energy to flow once more. This produces a great feeling of well being. More importantly yoga stills the Mind. It removes stress. You will be able to remember more if you are relaxed. It is a blissful state and very healing.

Being a discipline, the more practiced it is, the more beneficial and rewarding it is. Yoga classes are held almost everywhere and they are usually cheap to attend. With practice you can perform the exercises alone, so it is a free and effective means of treatment and prevention. Search the web for a yoga center using the word "yoga". If you are in the USA (especially), Argentina, Australia, Brazil, Canada, Denmark, England Germany, Iceland, India, Ireland, Netherlands, Portugal, Scotland or Sweden there's a very good site at http://yogasite.com/teachers.html which will give you a majority of yoga centers.

Chapter 10

—USING THE ENERGY OF THE ASTRAL BODY

10.1 FEAR

Take your power back from Fear and walk into Love. Love is the key to Fear. It can wipe out all Fear.

1. **Confront the Fear**. Go into a meditative state. Play through the scenario to the extreme. Pretend it is as bad as it can get. Then make it worse. Play it to the hilt. It's better to play it out in a meditation rather than in your reality.

2. **Assume that everything in your life is going wrong**. See your life as an avalanche of bad news and events collapsing all around you—go from one bad story to another, e.g. first you lose your jib, then your phone is disconnected and your cat dies on the way to the hospital etc. Go into a meditation and feel it all crumbling. Then you demand it to stop. Sense yourself rising above it all and look below as you see it all collapse. When it is finished collapsing, put it all back together, changing it slightly if you want to, then set yourself back down in the middle of it. It gives a message to your subconscious. It reduces Fear and you'll find you'll start rebuilding in your reality of the Outside World.

10.11   Steps to Rid Yourself of Fear

1.   **Admit it now**. Detail it. Ask yourself "what is it I'm afraid of?" If you can't detail the Fears then you are not ready to admit it or there isn't any Fear there.

2   **Feel sorry for yourself** for 10 minutes only. Don't go into Victimhood or Martyr. Time it. Don't do any thing else in this time. It's not easy to do "poor me" and nothing but "poor me" for 10 minutes.

3.   **Fill your Mind** with something irrational, e.g. ice cream melting, something mindless. Do if for a few minutes.

4.   **Stop everything** in a meditation. Step back and see the picture of your life. Step out of yourself.

5.   **See the Fear as the illusion** that it is. Something that is not to be taken seriously. A soap opera. Fear diminishes if you see it like this.

6.   In a meditation fill yourself with Love, hope and courage. **Let Love in the chakras** as light displacing the musky dirty Fear. Courage is the willingness to go after what you want, to take risks, to go out on a limb, to jump, to trust yourself.

10.12   Conquering Fear

10.121   If the Fear is an ACTUAL FEAR, e.g. "I am afraid that I am going to lose my job":

1.   **Get alone**. Get by yourself. Usually you want to do the opposite, e.g. get busy or sleep or get bored. That's hiding. Retreat briefly from the world and become alone.

2.   When alone **face your Fears**. If it is actual Fear—confront it, play it out in your Mind, work with it. Visualize the Fear occurring and play it right through to the end. Talk or write it out. Even talk to a friend literally or a mirror.

3.   **Look to see what the Fear is a symptom of**, i.e. what is the faulty belief that produces it—then change the belief.

4. **Play through the Fear again** many different ways—make it silly. Takes the edge off. In your Mind play silly music in the background to accentuate the unreality of it.

10.122 If it's a POTENTIAL FEAR (a Fear to which there is no real immediate likelihood), e.g. when I get old. Look at it as a symptom of what it might be. Then ask yourself "what belief is it a symptom of? Then do steps 2 to 4 above.

10.123 PERMISSION DECLARATION PHASE: Talk to yourself and give your self permission to conquer—to be free of the Fear. Then once free declare out loud "I am free...I have conquered this Fear". I forgive myself for having the Fear in the first place.

10.124 REMEDIES:

1. **Write a Fear letter:**
    Express your Fears on paper. Be detailed. Be specific. Very specific. Add in the color, the sound, what it looks like and keep writing. The next day re-read and qualify it. The following day burn it page by page and as it burns know your Fears all have been conquered. Writing stops the Mind. The object of the exercise is to stop the Mind.

2. **Water Technique**
    Fill 3/4 glass of water. Lie down. Hold the glass on the solar plexus (3rd chakra). Imagine your Fear going into the water. Play through the Fear and the story based on it. As your Mind wanders know it's your Ego that is doing this. Sense the ugly looking, feeling and sounding Fear going into the water. Then get up and flush the water down the toilet. Rinse the glass. 3/4 fill the glass again. Put it on your heart (4th chakra) and feel all the Love, joy and wonder, the people who Love you, safety. (What you focus on—is what you get. What you pay attention to is what you create). Sit up and drink 1/2 the water. 20 minutes later drink the rest and know that the Fear you felt has been replaced by the Love you have drawn to you. This is a ritual for the Mind.

10.2 ANGER

Anger is a most destructive emotion. Denied Anger will destroy you. You have a right to be angry. Some of you more than others. Unless you release this Anger though you can never be happy. You can never truly feel Love. And Love is really the only thing that you want. More than wanting to punish and to feel good about doing that, you want to be loved. That is what caused the hurt in the first place. You are not being asked to make friends with the people who hurt you. For some of you this would not be appropriate.

10.21 Meditate It Out

Find an Anger that you have that you want to work with. It may be with your mother from when you were 13 and she wouldn't let you go to the dance that with boy. At the time you couldn't express how you really felt—like you just wanted to kill her and you thought that she was the cruelest most hard hearted person who had no sensitivity to your feelings and needs. At the time though you couldn't express these feelings and thoughts and you buried the Anger, denied it or harbored it by telling your friends over and again about how terrible it was to grow up with your mother.

Write out the incident factually and in chronological order. First this happened, then that happened.

Go into your meditation and see yourself there as the 13 year old person in that chain of events. Play it through in your Mind to the end and feel the suppressed feelings and what it was like to feel them and then how you dealt with those feelings in such a way that they became suppressed or harbored.

Now replay the whole scene of events again only this time change it so that you express exactly how you feel, pour out the Anger, hit her, kill her, do whatever you would have done but felt that you could not. Say what you didn't say then.

Then after you come out of the meditation write a few lines on how it felt to do what you did. Then you can work with that. It may give you a reason why you still harbor the emotion. Often behind Anger you will find feelings of loneliness, hurt, disappointment, grief. The Anger masks these and it these deeper feelings that you need to be aware.

Only after you can really feel freedom can you know that you are done with that Anger. You may have to do the technique a few times to deal with a particular incident.

10.22 Write It Out

This is a very easy and effective technique. You write a letter to the person with whom you are angry. Do not give it to them—ever. That will get you into even more trouble and would cause more Anger. This is a technique that you are doing on yourself. They are just an outplay of your beliefs.

1. Start with "dear so and so, I am writing to tell you why I am angry with you". Or you may want to express exactly how you feel—like, "why I am so incredibly pissed off at you, you bastard is…I hate you for what you did to me."

2. Then just tell it like it is for you. Write it all out. All the detail. What you feel and think. And keep writing until you can't write any more.

3. When you have finished writing, fold the letter, put it in an envelope and hide it away out of sight.

4. The next day take out the letter and re-read it. This time make the letter stronger. Don't give them the benefit of the doubt. Remove the excuses for their behavior.

5. When you have finished writing, fold the letter, put it in an envelope and hide it away out of sight.

6. The next day take out the letter and re-read it carefully. Then page by page burn the letter.

These actions give your Sub-conscious a message of hiding the Anger, discovering it and then releasing it. When you feel that you are free of the weight of the Anger then your work is finished. You may need to do the technique a number of times on different people. Anger against one person could have its roots in the Anger towards another.

10.23   Talk It Out

Do this with someone who is close to you. It may not be appropriate to talk to the person with whom you are angry. Or use a tape recorder and rant and rave into it—as you might if you did an Anger letter. If using a tape listen to it three times then throw the tape away.

10.24   Processing It Out

You may want to speak directly to the person with whom you are angry. May I suggest the following process.

1. Set up a time with that person. Give them some space to prepare. Do not tell them that you are angry with them (they may already know anyway) but say that you want to talk to them about something that is concerning you and you do not want to mention it now. When they are free to talk you will talk about it then.

2. You should think about what it is that you want to talk to them about. Be clear. Don't just lob up at the meeting and start talking coming from every direction. Be focused. Do your homework. What are your pay offs in holding onto the Anger? Know where you are coming from. Know how the Anger is coming out in you—physically, in relationship etc.

3. Communicate openly and honestly in the dialogue. Take responsibility for what happened.

4. Look at the impact on them. How did your Anger affect them? What is happening for them in all of this?

5. Take responsibility for putting things right.

6.   This process will allow a new space in which to communicate with that person again.

10.3   SELF PITY

10.31   How Do I Process Self Pity?

1.   **Write out** the ways that you are in Self Pity.
2.   **Acknowledge** it for what it is. An illusionary game that you are choosing to play. You are not helpless or powerless. You choose to be in Self Pity.
3.   What are your **payoffs**? Write them down. I have listed some of the following. Be specific as to how Self Pity shows itself in your life—

   (a)   you get to avoid responsibility, impact and success
   (b)   you get to punish
   (c)   you get to feel righteous Anger
   (d)   you get to stay in Ego by asking it for a guarantee that it can't give the guarantee that you can get a better pay off if you give up Self Pity
   (e)   Self Pity itself—its warm and a nostalgic memory from childhood
   (f)   you get to feel self important—"poor me I'm caught in Self Pity"

10.32   Releasing Self Pity

Self Pity stops the magic and separates you from the Universe, your Higher Self, your health and your happiness. Consider the following dynamics—

1.   In Self Pity **you create a rationale** for it, e.g. you create too much work on your desk and too few hours to get it done in. As another example, you may blame unfair neighbors and use

your Victimhood to create the Self Pity—you attracted to you the unfair neighbors in the first place in order to create Self Pity. The pity came first, then the overwork and the neighbors. It was never the other way around. Sorry, but you create it all. I know how people in Self Pity HATE to hear that they are doing it to themselves. I should know. I used to do it to myself all the time.

2.   Others try to **use pity to transform** themselves, e.g. if I go far enough down, then the only way to go is up. Sorry that doesn't work either. Transformation occurs by way of Love, divinity, elegance, impact, intimacy, caring, worth, respect, clarity and excellence. Self Pity eliminates all of the transformers. It locks you in the old form.

3.   Being hooked on Self Pity you **won't ask or receive help or Love** because they are the antithesis of pity. Your task is to receive Love.

4.   You **don't want to admit** what your pity is. It is denial. I don't want to admit that those reasons are real. I don't want to tell myself the truth. Or, I don't want to acknowledge the impact of my pity, e.g. it is you who is the punisher. It is your story that "it is the others who like to punish, control, be arrogant and refuse to give it up". What you are really saying is that you like to punish, control, be arrogant and refuse to give it up and will not let go of that story. It sustains you and justifies your position.

Now that you understand what Self Pity is then you are now ready to be free of it.

1.   Think about the original **reason of how you began to feel sorry for yourself** and how that was a creative solution to an otherwise unsolvable problem. But that creative solution outlasted its effectiveness and has become noble, acceptable— almost pitiable. Then beneath it is a not so noble reason and there is a reason why you won't let go of your pity. You don't know what that is yet. Find out what the pay offs would have

been for the you that you were when you began to do Self Pity. They are probably the same now whenever the circumstances present themselves for you to go back into Self Pity. You see, you keep re-creating the same scenarios in your life, the same projections. They are all coming from the same beliefs. So whenever you find yourself in the same situation that you were when say you were a child, e.g. faced with an authority figure that wouldn't let you have your way, then you will repeat the pattern from that first time. So go into meditation and see yourself before you as a child and ask the child what it wants. Then give it to them in that meditation. In other words, put that piece of your Mind to rest and that aspect of you will no longer need to create an external reality to satisfy itself. As you create your own reality, until you become whole by healing the various parts of yourself, then these unwhole parts will continue to be discolored filters in your energy fields creating your life as a struggle.

2. **Decide not to take the payoffs any more**. Think of the potentials and opportunities that will be there without Self Pity. Remind yourself of how you are hurting yourself and destroying your life.

3. **Use a time-lapse approach**—feel Self Pity and only Self Pity for 20 minutes. Wallow in it. Don't think of another thing. (I bet you can't). That will wear it out and you too. It's almost impossible to do.

4. Become aware of **the pitfalls of Self Pity**. If you do then you can recognize when you are doing it and then just stop doing it. These are—
    (a)   becoming a Victim of Self Pity—"poor me"—a blamer
    (b)   you have forgotten that you create your own reality
    (c)   you use Self Pity as a defense—"but I was feeling sorry for myself because…" is no excuse.

5. **Draw up 3 columns**. One for the Victim, one for the winner and one for you. Look at the different aspects of your life—Love,

career, friends, your relationships and success. In the Victim column write down how a Victim would handle each particular aspect, e.g. leave the assignment to the last minute then cry "poor me" to his work mates the next day. The winners column write down how a winner would handle each particular aspect, e.g. thoroughly research the assignment well before hand in the library, the Net, book shops, in the field, then having done an assignment writing course, complete the assignment, have it bound and neatly printed and presented. Then in the 3rd column how you would do it. This is a good little exercise and one that can be applied to all aspects of your life.

10.4 MARTYRHOOD & VICTIMHOOD

10.41 How Do You Stop Martyr?

You can't be a little bit of a Martyr or a big Martyr. It is like pregnancy. You are either a Martyr or not. Martyrhood spreads—seeping through. In Martyr you are giving in to your Ego and your Ego is never satisfied. Because you are not wanting to feel gratitude, because you are hanging onto a fantasy and you are angry at the Universe, you want him to notice it, to fix it and only the Universe can do it.

To stop Martyr you have to make the decision to stop it. Cold turkey. Only you can make that decision. While so long as you are a Martyr you can never become aware of the different components of yourself, self awareness, being aware of your impact, your self worth. You have no basis of esteem and you are not being honest, having any integrity or being responsible, trustworthy. You are unable to listen to your inner voice or follow your emotional nature and your goal is to hurt others. Self Love is out of the question. You may be a narcissist—which is an obsession with an illusion, which keeps changing. Because of these things Martyrs can't be realized and because of that there can be no unconditional Love—the most beautiful Love of all. Vision, impeccability and elegance are out of the question. You can't be spiritual—you deny yourself a whole aspect of who you are and you can't heal if all of you can't be accessed and healed. This is what you are giving up in being a Martyr. YOU CAN'T BE YOURSELF. YOU CAN'T BE WHOLE. AND YOU CAN'T KNOW WHO YOU ARE.

Martyrs hurt people and you can never be spiritual and hurt people. Martyrs think that they are smarter because they are more sophisticated than Victims. You are being your Ego when you do Martyr and the role of your Ego is to kill you.

So when you find yourself doing Martyr (feeling misunderstood, hopeless, unappreciated, burdened etc.), STOP FOR A MOMENT and REALIZE THAT WHAT YOU ARE REALLY SAYING IS THAT—

1. you are not going to be spiritual and therefore not healed as a whole
2. you want to hurt people
3. you are going to be dumb and
4. you are not going to be yourself.

At what point do you decide that you are not going to do that? When it gets to be too much…unhappiness, sabotage, the crisis gets too big? You know it is time to give up Martyr. This is how—

1. **Figure out who it is that you want to punish**? And it isn't you either. You are the only one who doesn't get hurt by Martyr—although ultimately you do, because you are so dumb. Admit it. Don't be a coward. And the reason you want to punish them is because you are a Martyr. It is that simple. Coming up with a lot of reasons is only avoiding responsibility. The why is because you are angry and want revenge. STOP. Don't sigh, take that action that is needed—realize when you are in Martyr.

2. **Bust from that promise that the Ego has made to you.** As you get older the promises become more unlikely of happening. Let go of the promise and get angry at your Ego and punish it. How? Go into meditation and bust it. See Chapter 11 .1 on how

to do this. Bash it up. Slap it around. Kick it out of your reality. Your Martyr is coming from your Ego.

3. **Start to feel gratitude for having caught yourself in time**. Feel the Love, then and there.

4. **Start acting in a loving way**. Do something loving. There and then. Let yourself be loved.

5. **Start building a real future**. You pretend you don't know what it is but you do. A Martyr lives in the fantasy and blocks the real future. You really don't want the fantasy because you have not bothered to create a real future. That should be done at home ahead of time in preparation for when you next head into Martyr. Don't build the next reality on what you might have wanted it to have been but you aren't because of an excuse, e.g. "my parents wouldn't let me do (whatever it was) but if they had then now…" etc.

6. **Make friends with your Subconscious**. Let it work with you but you have to be in charge. Create new beliefs. Accept everything. Be willing to and look forward to experiencing what your Ego does not like. This is how you diffuse it, and clear the Shadow. Let your spiritual self be a witness, sense that self around you, watching what you are doing, thinking, behaving and when you are heading into Martyr watch it looking at you—"is this how I want to act in front of myself?" Use it as a motivation to stop. And then your Higher Self, Soul, the Universe becomes your witness. Imagine it as an angel if you wish.

7. Finally, if you can recognize that you are in Martyr, and that you have been powerful enough to create it, then recognize that and **just stop doing it**! Just stop it! Then and there. In time this is the only technique you will need to use. In time Martyr will happen less and less.

10.5 GUILT

10.51 How Do You Release Guilt?

1. What is causing the Guilt? Where did it come from? What is it for you? Are you using it for any of the purposes as to **why** you feel Guilty? What purpose is the Guilt serving? Let it sink in—realize that Guilt is not noble. It is deadly.

2. **Monitor** your Guilt for 7 days. Note about what you felt Guilty. Note the time of day and the incident. Then correlate the results. It can give you a clearer image of your Guilt, by monitoring. Work with the easiest Guilts first.

3. Work with the **Guilt of the child/adolescent** aspects of yourself. Go into a meditation and connect with those aspects to find out what it is. Express the Anger. Bring it to the surface. See the previous section 10.2 on how to release Anger.

4. Look for the **pay offs** and let them go.
    (a) What am I avoiding? Specifically what responsibility, success, creative expression.
    (b) Who are you punishing specifically? Emotional blockages always involve punishment.
    (c) Who gave you the message of Guilt that you would be betraying if you gave up Guilt? Parent, sibling, teacher? Who did you make the promise to?
    (d) Why is the Anger held righteously? What is the Ego saying? What is the Ego's guarantee? It wants to know "If I give up Guilt will I still be able to control, not be depressed, better than, hide, expect others to do it for me."
    (e) What do I feel sorry for myself about?
    (f) What stroke of self importance do I get?
    (g) What do I get to hang on to? What do I lose if I give up Guilt?

5. **Convert Guilt to the Anger** that it really is, then process the Anger and release it. Anger release includes hitting a pillow with a baseball bat, punching a punching bag.

6. **Develop character, ideals and principles.**
    IDEALS=those things for which you seek which are intangible and abstract. Higher focus in life, e.g. searching for Love, the spark of energy in mankind, compassion.
    PRINCIPLES=positive boundaries, honesty, integrity, responsibility. They are based on ideals.
    CHARACTER=adherence to principle.
    With the Guilt gone the void needs to be filled with CHARACTER, *which* in turn is based on principle.

7. Imagine what life would be like if you did not feel Guilt. Start visualizing that.

1 to 5 happen in your time as you allocate time to them. 6 and 7 happen over the rest of your life. It's on going.

10.6   OPENING TO YOUR FEELINGS

If you want to know what emotions you are stuffing down in your body and won't feel then slowly start to stop taking the numbing agents and stop the numbing behaviors. Those emotions are trying to tell you something about your beliefs, your negativity, your blockages and your disease. This is the first step on the path to knowing who you are—take away the smoke screen and the illusion that you hide behind. You start becoming aware as the anesthetic wears off. You begin to recognize the feelings that come up and deal with them—Self Pity, Anger, Guilt, Fear, not good enough, deservability, Love, joy, happiness. Recognize where you are feeling them. Then release those feelings using any of the number of relevant techniques described in this book or referred to in other sources.

Sometimes addictions can be to other things. When you feel the obsessive feelings/addictive streak, sit with the feeling. There is a hole in a chakra that needs filling. So ask, "what am I feeling under this?", e.g. Anger, Fear, Self Pity or what? And under that what are you feeling? e.g. hurt, betrayal, Fear, Anger or what? And why? Ask and then go into the feelings. Ask yourself, "if I go and do this thing I feel compelled to do, will it make me feel better, is it just a band aid, or is it me just getting me so pre-occupied so that I don't have to deal with it any more?" Keep going deeper each time it comes up. It is trying to say something to you.

Addictiveness and obsession are related. Obsession is the treadmill of the Ego. Pull back.

Ask yourself "What am I creating here? Is there another way?", e.g. through grace and elegance.

Ask yourself: "Do I deserve this?" if not ask, "Why am I doing it then?" This may be because in your Mind you think that you have been really bad.

Ask yourself "Why have you been so bad?" It may be because you don't fit in. That you are different to others.

Ask yourself "why am I different?" This may be because you have different ideas. "Why are they different?" Keep going deeper and deeper within your feelings. Keep talking to the voice within. Then call on your Higher Self to be present. That energy will help you deal with anything that comes up in this process. Get a psychic counselor if you can't get the answers.

These little steps add up to big ones. Always keep going deeper. Pluck out the belief and create a new one. Your life will change. You will have time and it will bring you joy and move you beyond just getting caught in survival. Your life now is probably a major exhausting battle. Do you get tired easily? Are you always tired at the end of the day?

In the *Celestine Prophesy* we were shown how a person's energy connected with another person or thing. We are drawn to objects of power. We not only draw power from it but we give power to it. Objects of addiction are a good example or a person we may have seen in a supermarket with which we have "fallen in Love" on sight. An addict no longer has the use of their reasoning Mind. The power object is everything. The object now controls them. Usually the need is emotional. With these people their Self Esteem is linked directly to the power object. It is harder for the person who has given their power away to heal because healing involves active power. In these cases they can only surrender to a greater power and allow themselves to be filled with that power—the power of Love.

So what we have to do is to re-direct our power.

1. To do that we have to get in touch with our emotional needs. One way to do that is to say no to the addiction. I've spoken of this earlier.

2. Think of yourself as an energy being not just as a physical being. Your energy is recording your experience. Take a good look at what energy is in your life—every day.

3. With practice you can become so self aware that you feel which part of your physical body is not up to scratch. With your eyes closed just bring your attention to each of your chakras, one at a time, and feel what is there. Joy or pain?

4. If you are losing power, ask yourself why.

5. Ask what draws your power—not who. If it is a person, then they will be reflecting back to you the part of yourself that you do not accept, i.e. your Shadow. You need to learn the lesson that the person has for you. You are in blame (=Victim) if you think that they are the cause of your unhappiness.

6. Think of illness as a power disorder. Feeling Victimized only adds to your illness. You need to be active in order to heal. Support all aspects of who you are.

Chapter 11

—Using The Energy Of The Mental body

11.1 REIGNING IN THE NEGATIVE EGO

11.11 Dealing With Ego

Do this exercise—look at what you think your "better thans" are. Be specific (the Ego loves being vague) about the two biggest, e.g. I am a guru, I know all, I am the best in my field, I always win, I am the most handsome. Then look at the type of message that you are putting out and decide which of the 5 types you tend to use most frequently. The 5 types being—

1. I can do it all by myself—I don't need anyone (a cause of AIDS—defensiveness).
2. Somebody else has to do it for me.
3. I am the best—I am the worst: it is always one extreme or the other—all comparisons of best are made from a place of Ego.
4. I am evolved, there is nothing more that I have to learn—I am so un-evolved, I couldn't possibly learn.
5. I always make mistakes, I can never do anything right, I am perfect.

There are two ways to deal with Ego. Release it or bust it. Where you can prove factually the "better than" or "worse than" then you should release it.

11.12   Releasing The Negative Ego

To heal the Ego you RELEASE that part of it which is hurting you and others. Actions based on matters of fact are, e.g. the "better than" of being more intelligent. If you don't have the evidence to prove it then that is a crazy one to have. All crazy "better thans" should be released.

1. **List the better thans**—all of them. Pick the one that you want to work with. Overlay these better thans with the reality that you created yourself (just accept for the moment that you created all your realities).

2. **Look at the hurt that you have done** in the name of your Ego—specifically that which you have done with others so as to concentrate on hurting yourself and having Self Pity (the Ego gorges on it). Own the hurt for what it is.

3. **Dealing with the pay offs**. Ask yourself
   - what do you get to avoid,
   - who do you get to punish,
   - what do you do with the rightness that the Ego gives you,
   - what do you get as a guarantee,
   - how much do you get as enjoyment from the Self Pity, self importance,
   - what are you afraid to loose, e.g. the treasured past with the selective nostalgia, being a child, adolescent, the hey-day of your life?

4. **Forgive yourself** for the hurt you have done, for being so stubborn in taking the pay offs.

5. Decide **what you want instead**—being nice to people, friendly, jovial and start living that 10 minutes at a time. Be more caring for people perhaps. Your Ego will want to set you

up by wanting you to be the new person forever and you will not be able to or you will start getting better thans because you did. So watch that and do not get sucked in by it and then defeated when it happens—back under the control of Ego. Start with 10 minutes, then an hour, and then a day at a time. Remember that you are your Ego. It is not a separate entity that you can cut off and throw away. Without Ego you are dead. You are just healing an aspect of yourself.

6.   Start **feeding your conscious self**—starve the Ego and it will shrink back to its normal size. Do it by using the positive feedback to stretch further, to see further, to lift the fog.

7.   Let yourself **be more than you are**—be aware of yourself as a metaphysical/spiritual being and not just human. Add another dimension to yourself. See yourself as part of a bigger picture. You are part of bigger picture. Knowing who you are is all about discovering the pieces that you didn't know existed. It is about becoming complete. In getting in touch with this spiritual aspect you are not denying your physical self—if anything you embrace that just as much—you can be physical and spiritual at the same time. Being spiritual doesn't mean that you can't enjoy yourself with sex and drugs and rock and roll. Being aware means that you are now free to choose just how much enjoyment you really want—because now there is all of you choosing and not the limited aspect of Ego which previously ran your life. Your priorities will change as you become more whole. There will be a deep sense of satisfaction with your daily life and it will blossom and grow beautifully. It really will. It's hard to explain the experience. But there will be a shift as you go up a level in your maturity. It is nothing to be afraid of. In fact it is immensely and richly rewarding. The Fear you feel is coming from that part of your Ego, which hates change and knows that it will loose control if you become all of who you really are. There is a large chunk of you that you

haven't been in touch with before. A chunk that you need to get in touch with if you want to be truly happy.

Releasing Ego is a continual process. You have to do it every day. Eventually the boulder that your Ego has become will return to being a pebble that you can step over or kick out of the way in a second when it rears it pip-squeak head. Until then though your Ego will sell you out in a minute and tell you anything. It lies all the time. All the time. It has the capacity to undo in a second, a lifetime's work. That lapse of judgment—just ask Monica Lewinsky and Bill Clinton.

11.13   Busting the Negative Ego

Bust that part of the Ego which is destroying you. Actions based on states of being should be busted, e.g.

- a better than of attractiveness (unless you won an award for, i.e. there is evidence that you are more attractive, in which case it would be an action and something to be released as you can hold onto it),
- a better than based on your astrology/numerology
- hereditary
- family status
- your gender
- racial genetics
- quantity of money owed or owned.

Where you have tried to release it and it has not worked then bust it. Busting is a structure not a process.

1. You need to **understand the extreme of the Ego's fantasy** and where it takes you. The fantasy of the Ego is the worst possible reality that you can think, e.g. where the better than is "I am more intelligent" the worst case reality could be that you go insane because you are ahead of your time and they lock you up. "Isn't that sad," your Ego says. And in comes Self Pity to feed the Ego. Usually it means rising to the top, being

recognized and then in a great melodrama of the highest kind, going insane.

If the better than is to have money, then the worst case scenario would be to end up a bum on the street begging. There is nothing more dramatic than the rise and fall of great wealth. Look at the entrepreneurs of the 1980's that ended up in jail, sick, bankrupt, complicated in conspiracies or dead in the early 1990's when we had the worst recession since 1929. I am not saying that their failed realities were the product of Ego fantasy but it seems to fit the criteria. It could have been from Shadow. But I know for sure that their beliefs underscored the event.

If the better than is that you are the greatest Lover—the worst case scenario would be to end up impotent—not even Viagra would help, with a sexually transmitted disease, AIDS. Anything that would stop you having sex.

And for the person who thinks that they are the most spiritual the reality would be to be taken over by the "dark forces".

For the person who is loving then they could end up evil. You get the idea, yes? Look at your Fears and these will be your clues as to what you don't want to happen. They are the opposite to what your Ego is trying to convince you that you should have in order to be happy. If you are having your better than out of Fear as a motivator then it is a good starting place to look. If you are hanging onto your fantasy then you want to be destroyed by the opposite to it. This is how your Ego is trying to kill you by tricking you and appealing to your lack of self worth and Self Esteem. If you can be the best then you will be deserving and will be rewarded and loved. Ego knows that you need Love and will promise you all sorts of ways to get it—but it will NEVER deliver on any of them. Waking up is being self aware. Please see that by being asleep to who you are can only give you unhappiness and a sense of failure and incompleteness. If you can remember day dreaming about how grand it would be if…and you were wishing for it to be true—a complete fantasy—then start to own it as a fantasy and realize that within it is the seeds of your destroyer.

2.   Let yourself **feel it** and really start to get scared. Experience it meditatively. Play it out to its worst. Better to live it out in the painlessness of a dream than to live it. As you get scared realize that is where you are heading and who you are going to hurt and take with you on the way.

3.   **Be responsible for it**—and see how you are doing with it. See how you and your Ego are functioning such as to bring about that destruction—the money you are foolishly spending to go broke, the unsafe sex, the business decisions based on what other people might think of you, an unfeeling nature that loses friends. Realize that you are doing it step by step. Own that. There will be an inner feeling that you will know already that you are doing it.

4.   **Make** the decision, the choice and in a meditation visually **blast the reality**, not the Ego, that you are moving towards and feel the impact of blasting the future reality.

The follow up then becomes the same as for releasing. Decide how you want to be, feed the consciousness, be more than the physical being. As the fantasy keeps trickling back, keep busting it and it will becomes less and less.

11.14 The Positive Ego

This is the message deliverer that it should be. The interface. You can't see it. Develop it further—it helps to negate the Negative Ego.

1.   **Think.** Easier said than done. We have been trained not to think but to respond. Put some time aside each day. Twenty minutes to an hour is good and think about what you thought that day. It can be stimulated by reading fiction and non-fiction –stay away from the glossy magazines which drip with the Ego of better than and how to be better than—at least in

their opinion. Save these as resources for creativity and see them for what they really are. Think abstractly about something that will need a conclusion or think about a concept that you have not thought about before and if you want to write down what you have thought about. A mindless non thinking person is fertile ground for the Negative Ego.

2.   Look for the **joy** in your day. And search for the joy and decide to find more joy than the day before.

3.   Look for the **lovingness**.

4.   Look for the **ease**. How easily could you have lived today? How much more easily could you have lived today? What less hassles could you have had? What could have gone more smoothly?

5.   Look for the **laughter** for you are the silliest thing in your reality that day. Also at the silliest that goes on around you. Did you laugh today or do something to make yourself laugh today?

6.   **Evaluate your point of view**. Where are you looking to or from? There are basically 3 windows to look through—

   a.   the Ego

   b.   the subconscious

   c.   the Unconscious.

   Looking through the window of the Ego is looking at the past, at what might have been. Here you are basing your future on the past and you are only seeing the promise of a future. The future never comes. It is always in the future. You are in the now.

   Looking through the subconscious will give you a metaphysical reality that you create.

   Looking through the Unconscious lets you have hope, Love, the sense of being more than just an animal, stretching yourself into the void and appreciating the moment and your moreness.

7.   **Loving**. Through loving yourself and others you disarm the Ego and starve it. This is where you want to be. The answer is always Love. If in doubt about anything, if you don't now what to do—Love is the answer. What is Love and all those

things you know? Division III is all about clearing your block-ages so that you can receive Love.

18—21 years are the most powerful time for the growth of the Negative Ego. Here adolescence embarks on adulthood. There is a lot of Fear present as you move out into the world having to prove yourself and being accepted. You are on the brink of facing the world alone and realize that you don't know anything, that you faked it with your Ego and you've been bluffing. At this age you were least able to function on your own, to think, to Love, to look at the complexity of life and it was the time that you were most afraid of loneliness—the original Fear from which all Fears come. Go into a meditative state and look at this age. You might remember things and events and people that you forgot. Look at how your Ego was working in those circumstances. Apply the 5 types of Ego described in 6.11 so that you can see where you have been coming from.

11.2   HEALING BELIEFS, ATTITUDES AND CHOICES

Even though beliefs are what our reality is built on it is the one area that the least can be said about. Beliefs can't be changed. Once they are in the subconscious they are there for good. You can't erase this soft-ware. You can choose though not to run it. Like all software you can create later versions. If for instance you run a particular program of beliefs when at a party where you know no one, then create a new form of beliefs. The trick is to be consciously aware of the old pattern and knowing what your beliefs. Don't be told that this is hard to do. That is the belief of the person who is giving you that story and more importantly it is you creating a person in your reality who is reflecting back to you your own beliefs about how hard it is.

Earlier in the book I explained how to discover what your beliefs are. If you like you can go into a meditation and imagine going into a room in which there is your Book of Beliefs. Open this. Tear out the page with the old belief on it. Throw that page onto the fire in the fire place near the table, then turning to a blank page write out the new belief that you want to have. Beliefs usually start with the words "I am" and are voiced in the present tense. If you have any trouble in knowing what new things to believe just read Louise Hay's *You Can Heal Your Life*. It's full of wonderful affirmations. I read her book in the mid to late 1980's and I still often see copies of it in the homes of people. It is a classic book for self awareness.

Do *The Work* of Byron Catie. This is the best way to deal with beliefs in all their forms. The answer is that simple. I have no connection with Byron Catie. I have never met her or spoken to her or corresponded with her. I just know that her techniques work. They did for me and on many people who I saw using them in Europe. It's really good stuff.

Power is essential for healing and maintaining health. Attitudes that generate a feeling of powerlessness not only lead to low Self Esteem, but also deplete the physical body of energy and weaken overall health.

If your body is a history book of your experiences, then you must be in some way responsible for having created the illness. "They did it to me" is only an excuse—I don't care how elaborately you have created the them doing it to me story. It won't wash any more. No more Self Pity for you. It doesn't serve you. You let "them" do it to you. You put yourself in a place where they could. You invited them in with your energy. At some time you are going to have to take responsibility for what happened to you. Resisting that will not help you either—nor obviously will it make it any easier for you. In fact it will only make the pain greater. You have to give up the addiction to the pain. You are using it to stay addicted to the numbing agents.

For some people it may be hard to own up to what happened to you in your life because all along you thought that you were the innocent one. And in being innocent that you would get the rewards of Love and attention. This was your pay off. Now for the first time you are seeing your reality for what it is. The evidence of your beliefs is your experience and it is plainly in front of you. It may also be evidence of how much you don't like yourself or the extremes that you will go to in order to get the Love that you want. If you don't like you then you will create situations in your life to prove how unpopular you are. This could even mean getting yourself mugged. Harsh? Not if you think about it. Logical in fact. Perhaps this may start to explain why you weren't the popular one at school or at work. You were excluding yourself with your beliefs about yourself.

11.3   CASTING LIGHT ON THE SHADOW

The basis of the 4 day workshop that I completed in Los Angeles with Lazaris can now be found in a hands-on work book/journal. This has specific written exercises to take you through the Fears that are in your Shadow and then bring you out into the other side of your Shadow where you have also hidden the beauty, Love and abundance that you spend so much of your life searching for. It was in you all along. Underneath the slime of that part of you which you judged as not being very nice, there is that part of you which you know is really a very nice person. A very lovable person. For most people it is the innocence of childhood. Here in your denial it lies waiting to be uncovered and brought back into the light. Once exposed and freed you can use that energy to attract to you others who are also living a life of beauty, Love and abundance. They will reflect your beauty, Love and abundance back to you and then you will begin to see a substantial and marked change in your life and the people who are in it.

Now is probably a good time to give you a warning. A guide to look out for. Until now everything in your life has been a reflection of your beliefs. And this won't change. But the reflections back to you will change. Do not be alarmed if you have a huge fight with your best friend. Do not be alarmed if you go bankrupt. Do not be alarmed if your spouse leaves you or your pet dies. Do not be alarmed if you change jobs. Do not be alarmed if you become ill. These are extreme examples of what happens when you change fundamental beliefs. Beliefs that have been serving your Ego and not you. The more radical you change the more radical your reality will around you. Some of you are craving that I know. Others of you will want to go more gently. In most cases though once you tap into beauty, Love and abundance the energy will carry you along at a pace comfortable to you. Remember that these places, things and events in your life are only there because you believe they are there. Change is inevitable. The more you resist you more it is going to impact on you when it comes. It could go to the very core of your being. It is nothing to be afraid of. It is part of the process of "out with the old. In with the new". As you change so too will the people around you. Some of the people you know will stop treating you in a particular way and start treating you another and usually more pleasing way. Others will just leave. Your own behaviors will change towards other people too. As you step into your power—and so much of it is in your Shadow—these shifts will begin to occur. At the end of the day though you are gong to be so much more than what you are now and so much more happy. Just keep going. Don't look back. It is a journey of self discovery that you are on. There is light at the end of the tunnel and it is the light that you are seeking.

Please remember that the Universe never gives you anything to deal with that you are not ready to deal with. Even if you don't think you are. And if you choose not to deal with it then it will come back to you at a later time. Eventually you will have to deal with it. It is part of your denial and so it is inescapable because it is you anyway. Sometimes when it does come back it is bigger than it was the time before. That is how denial works. So in your changing "life-scape" the scenes will change.

The Lazaris material is entitled *The Shadow Workbook* and is published by NPN Publishing Inc. in 1995 for Concept:Synergy the promoter of the Lazaris material. You should refer to their web site at www.lazaris.com for information on ordering this "must have" book. Chapters include the Truth about the Shadow, Owning the Shadow,

Engaging the Shadow, Making Peace with the Shadow, Creating the Alliance, Regaining the Energy. You will get to see the disguises that the Shadow wears and how the qualities of the Shadow are reflected in our families and the people whom we are intimate with in our lives— as well as our exaggerated emotions and the repeated negative and positive feedback that seems to follow us everywhere.

An alternative and more in depth analysis is in the book *Fear No Evil. The Pathwork Method of Transforming the Lower Self* by Pierrakos and Donovan Thesenga by the Pathwork Foundation Inc printed in 1993. Here Pierrakos explores the Lower Self which is kept hidden by aspects of your personality called the Mask Self and the Idealized Self Image—these are glorified images of what you think you are and what you pretend to be. The book is quite advanced and one often used by professionals. All the same it is readable and is not caught up using psychological terminology. The book also goes into aspects of healing the child part of you. A lot of childhood stuff gets shoved into the Lower Self so it is important if you want to spend intense time in this part of your psyche to look at the Child aspect. It talks about the need to feel all feelings and the Fear of feeling all feelings. That is why those feelings are in the Shadow in the first place.

In your refusal to feel because of your numbness this allowed the Shadow to grow. Your denied Fear went into Shadow. If you stay numb and refuse to know your Emotional Body, you will never be able to feel the power and blessings of Love but rather be condemned to living in a Fear based reality.

Chapter 12

—USING THE ENERGY OF THE CAUSAL BODY

12.1 THE HIGHER SELF AND CONSCIOUSNESS

Your Higher Self does not need to be healed. It is perfect already. You just need to connect with it. It is Love. This will foster and support you. It is part of who you are just as your Shadow and Ego are. It is not a separate entity. It is the very best of you. Being in direct contact with the Universe that energy alone is sufficient to bring it into the light, to make you whole, you give you self awareness and to heal you. So it is a case of getting in touch with this aspect of who you are. And that is what needs fixing here. Your connection to spirit. Opening a pathway to let that energy in so that it may flow down into your life.

Look at these spiritual truth –
- Live what you believe
- Life is a learning process
- Positive energy is the most effective
- Live now—practice forgiveness
- Only you can make yourself happy—it is your responsibility to do so
- Change is constant—go with the flow.

In all spiritual beliefs God or the Great Power (what I have been calling the Universe) is seen as having the best of our human qualities. The old Christian way of seeing us as being in a God/Child relationship is coming to a close. Spiritual maturation is happening now. People generally are waking up to their spiritual connection. We are not dependent on the Universe but co-create with it. We are in the energy of the Universe and are part of the Universe, intricately woven into it—like PC's and lap tops all connected to the main frame computer—or what is now known as the world wide web. The Internet has become the perfect analogy for our relationship with the Universe. Our reality is once again reflecting our relationship with the universe.

Our life's purpose is to understand and develop the power of our spirit. This power is vital to our mental and physical well being. Abusing it siphons out the life force, we grow weak, become diseased and then die.

Shows such as Star Trek and Star Gate (and all science fiction shows and children's fantasies) are designed to open our Minds to the possibilities of the Universe. This genre of science makes it plausible for us to see and understand the unknown and the imaginative. Science serves as a means to an end. The point here is just because we can't imagine or know how something can be done does not mean that it can't be done.

A few examples—

(1)   when John F Kennedy made it his mission to place a man on the moon by 1969, the know how was all theory and some of it wasn't even thought of, but the mission was achieved.

(2)   no one could break the four minute mile for years, and then after it was broken a host of people broke it very quickly afterwards—almost in a matter of days in some cases. Athletes are looking to break the 3 minute mile but how it will be done is not known.

(3)   after Hilary and Tensing climbed Mt. Everest hundreds have followed.

The point is that once the way has been shown the path becomes very easy. This book attempts to show you the way by cutting through the volumes of information available to you elsewhere, by condensing it, giving you the big picture of the subject and referring you to texts for more detailed information. This book is guide or map.

We are at once separate from the Universe and part of it. This explains the concept of the Trinity—Father, Son and Holy Ghost. Each is separate but each is at the same time One or whole. Indivisible. We are the same with the Universe. The Ego separates us but keeps us connected at the same time.

By accepting yourself as you are, the less you are threatened by the differences of those around you, therefore the less you need to be separate or frightened of them. Love lets you be self accepting. Fear can't exist where Love is present. With less Fear there is more inner peace and that is reflected out into the world as more peace in the world.

12.2   BECOMING YOUR HIGHER SELF

We can consciously connect with the higher vibrations of our being—through meditation—to the place where there resides ultimate knowing, ultimate imagination, ultimate intuition, ultimate peace, ultimate Love, ultimate power, ultimate abundance, ultimate healing, ultimate stillness, ultimate joy and ultimate everything. Think about it. The Universe contains all that was ever known and experienced and by accessing it everything in the Universe can be yours. You don't need to take ecstasy because you will be in a state of ecstasy naturally. You won't have to get high because you will be in that state naturally and you will have access to the greatest and most imaginative Mind there is—your own as it is a reflection of the Universal Mind. There is only one Mind. And we all share it. The good thing about consciousness altering drugs is that they open your Mind by removing the man made, societal, emotional, Egoic and painful blockages that stop you from imaging anything outside your own little world. If you have had ecstasy then you know what it feels like to live without Fear and to be in a state of unconditional Love. You can get this high naturally by being all of who you are. When you are and you feel ecstasy then you will now you have arrived. This is experience talking here. These drugs can be used as tools. It's when they are misused that you have trouble. This is obvious.

In her book *Spiritual Growth: Being Your Higher Self* (printed by H J Kramer Inc in 1989) Sanya Roman demonstrates Reaching Upward, Opening Inward and Expanding Outward while she describes and gives techniques on how to become your Higher Self, raise your vibration, create using light, calm your emotions, link with your higher will, receive revelations and move into higher consciousness. She has already done the work. It is not the purpose of this book to restate her book here. I recommend the book to you instead. In fact all her books are very good.

12.3 LOVE

The Beatles, in one of their many songs about Love, said it all when they said "Love is the answer" and in another famous song "all you need is Love, Love. Love is all you need." And they were right. Its that simple. There's nothing more to say—having a better life is all about Love.

12.31 How Do You Love Yourself?

The qualities of Love are the means of loving. Go back to Chapter 7.4 to refresh yourself about these.

1.   What are you going to give of yourself? What are you going to give to yourself? Start doing it, e.g. money, money on yourself or more time.
2.   Care for yourself. Develop a project that is going to help you grow. Devote time to it. This is going to make such a difference.

3. Be more honest with your responsibility to yourself. You let your Ego function. It is you. Work at your ugly side. **Feel**.

4. **Assess yourself as an emotional being**. If the outside world that you see is an illusion then the only thing that is real is the energy that you feel, i.e. your emotions. All else that describes you is illusion—rich, clever, good looking etc. If you can't feel you can't self accept. If you try to numb an emotion you numb them all. They are interlinked. You can't freeze one end of an ice block.

5. **Know yourself**. Give yourself room for spiritual growth, e.g. meditation. Give yourself a chance to become alive and to discover. You' have punished and hurt yourself to find out who you are. You have already been the sadist and masochist to yourself.

6. **Be humble**.

7. Ask yourself "what is the **courageous** thing to do?" You are not standing still. You are either in Ego or in loving. How do you develop courage? By understanding courage and taking risks for the sheer joy of it not for the Ego's promise of being better than.

    As you apply these you'll come to a state of peace. This is a self awareness, self worth, Self Esteem, Self Love and self confidence. **Self Love is the key**. Move into it and through it. So having applied the above steps to yourself then apply them to other people.

12.32 Self Esteem

Given the emphasis on perfection, performance and form in the world that is continually dished up to us by the advertising industry, and in columnists and fashion's judgments of "what's in" and "what's out" it is no surprise that lack of Self Esteem is such a big problem. It is rooted in the very fabric of the person and has an historical basis that is imbued from childhood. Self Esteem can only improve as Self Love increases and you stop buying into the empty promises of the Negative Ego and the comparative judgments that it makes between you and the other whom you have judged as better than or worse than on the simplistic basis of what they look like or where they live or work.

So how can you feel good about yourself?

With cases of low Self Esteem the major source of distress comes from three areas:—

1.   Guilt.
2.   Lacking deserving.
3.   Self Esteem; or a combination of the three.

Self Esteem has to do with the Love that is earned as opposed to the Love that is given.

It is an elusive concept because:—

1.   It is a value judgment; because we were erroneously taught that judgments were bad esteem remains mysterious because esteem is a judgment. To judge we are told is bad, wrong, punishable, which in turn are three judgments of judging. Judgment hurts the people you do it to and you. So the issue becomes do you want to hurt or not? It is not a matter of right or wrong but do you want to hurt? Value judgments, however, are the relative placements of discernment, opinion and evaluation. So it is important to value judgment and care should be taken in making this distinction from the judgments of the Ego, which are based on being better than or worse than that which is being judged.

2.   It involves emotional estimates and subjective estimations. Every feeling you have is affected by your level of esteem, reflection of your esteem and is produced out of your esteem. Every thought is motivated out of and is a product of your esteem.

In the hierarchy of needs it is often placed and has the priority of being fourth. The priority of your needs is as follows—

1.   Survival needs
2.   Security needs

3. Belonging needs

4. Esteem. There is no beginning or end to esteem. Esteem is part of all four priorities. We are also taught not to have needs. Fill the needs. Some people re-label needs and call them preferences or wants. But there are certain needs and it is OK to have them. I need water. I need food. Needs fulfilled=happiness. Once fulfilled re-label them as "needs fulfilled". Move beyond needs fulfilled into preferences. It is these that will provide joy. Some problems come from calling preferences needs when they are not needs, e.g. I must have a man. I need a man. Correct labeling solves the problem and then you fulfill as necessary. Esteem is a need. And when called a want it is often foregone.

You never do not experience it. You are always dealing with it. Like a fish does not understand water, you do not understand esteem because you are part of a set that is constantly surrounded by issues of esteem but unlike the fish, you can learn about it.

12.321 Why is esteem so important?

1. Life is about growing. To learn to have fun, to consciously create success, to encounter, to confront and deal with yourself and to find out who you are. For it to occur you need a reason to explore and understand—esteem is the motivation.

2. Reality turns on belief and choice. As we have seen earlier the raw materials for reality creation are belief—out of which all other sources evolve and reality manifests. Beliefs are thoughts that we believe.
   - Attitudes are the lenses through which you choose to look at the world.
   - Feelings come as a result of attitudes.
   - Decisions are generated from them.
   - Choices are generated from decisions.
   - The new choices produce new thoughts, beliefs, attitudes, feelings and decisions.
   - The turning points are beliefs and choices.

So thinking differently, new attitudes, feelings are fine but unless they are strong enough to create a belief no change occurs. Choices motivate and esteem moves them to new beliefs i.e. your sense of evaluative estimate of yourself. Your esteem motivates the choices and beliefs. Reality comes from beliefs. Esteem gives you the willingness to explore, understand and to change.

3.   In many ways the human is the least prepared to deal with the world. Physically ill equipped, it is your ability to think and feel that distinguishes you from the animal and plant kingdoms. You can reason and so have dominion in the kingdoms. In order to productively and to progressively think and feel, it is important to be able to measure your impact and to be motivated out of a self appraisal and to have a sense of value. Esteem provides that measure and motivation and value.

4.   Every power of mine as a human comes from self evaluation. If you did not have it you will not grow and you would adopt the beliefs of others and shrink and render yourself powerless. You would not survive feeling that you are not fit to live and that thought would lead to death. Esteem is essential to existing. Without it you die—this is why Self Esteem is such a huge issue with AIDS. Not a lot of gay men in the 80's had high esteem.

12.322   What is esteem?

The evaluation, you make of yourself. The estimation. The appraisal. A value judgment that you make and adhere to. Esteem is the Love you earn upon which you value your right to exist as opposed to the Self Love you are given.

Esteem is comprised of several components each of which is important by itself. But when they are combined the combination produces a transmutation and a transformation that is Self Esteem.

12.323   What are the components of Self Esteem?

1. **A determination to be powerful.** Power is the ability to act. The determination to be willing and able to act regardless of anything. No matter how good or bad you may think it is.

2. **The ability to think and feel.** This does not mean how well you think as in your IQ or grades at school—they reflect what the teacher wanted to hear or your ability to repeat what was said. How able are you to think? e.g. in athletes—practice makes perfect. So in life practice thinking. Stretch your capacity. Develop it. Or do you take it for granted? Can you evaluate it? How have you developed your depth of feeling? What is your ability to feel and identify it? e.g. if you ran from Anger more than Love there would be less wars. You are suspicious of Love. The more terrifying emotions are the ones that society says are OK. Do you practice your emotions? Do you ever stop and think about what you have just seen on TV? How does it make you feel? If capacity is not developed you stop growing. A thinking Mind discourages the grasp of the Negative Ego.

3. **The evaluation of your character.** Esteem is an evaluation of your character. What is character? Character is comprised of several components:—

   i) The ideals that you hold. These are the essences or energies that you seek knowing that you will never fulfill them totally—truth, honesty, creativity, Love unconditionally. And although you will never acquire them all you know that you will become more because of your stretch/search for them. They add substance and depth to a person and allow more Love to be attracted.

   ii) With the ideals you establish principles—boundaries and levels of your identity. Character is the frequency with which you implement your principles. Without ideals and principles it is difficult to appraise your character. That is the basis of your Self Esteem. If the principles are not applied, e.g. open disclosure only when it is to your advantage then you lack character. The evaluation of your character is an ingredient in your esteem.

4. **A willingness and desire to seek understanding and meaning** and to allow perception and conception—to conceive something new. To seek is active. To allow is passive. How willing are you to understand and to see?

5. **The evaluation of principle** based on action versus expedient based action. Are your actions based on principles/ideals or what ever you can get away with/serve your agenda/easiest to do right now? Your estimation of this is what you determine your Self Esteem upon.

6. **Ability to integrate thought and feeling**. That you feel something does not always mean that there is a thought or fact behind it. All feelings are legitimate in that you feel them. Do they come from correct thinking/sounded in accurate thinking? e.g. you are frightened does not mean that there is something to be frightened of, but to deny that you feel frightened would be a mistake because you do feel it—regardless of whether or not you have a logical or valid reason for doing so. You then integrate to come up with action and evaluation of that action. How effective are you at integrating? e.g. can you get past emotion or do you let it ruin your day? If so, the thoughts and feelings aren't integrated. Make your beliefs on the basis of the integration.

7. **The determination that you are not helpless** regardless how bleak it may look. You can always ask for help. You can always find a solution even if you cannot see a solution now nor understand your position.

These seven components make Self Esteem. Your appraisal of your fitness to exist, to be powerful, to be filled with thought and feeling with character, understanding and perceiving, acting on principle, integrating thought and feeling and creating your own reality. That is what esteem is. You will always seek esteem. If you do not seek Self Esteem you will then seek false esteem such as being judged by how you look, what you wear, where you eat, where you live, where you work, what you drive—all the things of the illusion in which you live. Obviously then if you loose your looks (getting old will do it) then you would loose your esteem. Hello plastic surgery industry for many people who don't accept themselves as they are. There are exceptions as to why people would have this surgery. Not many though.

12.324 False esteem

The ways in which you will seek false esteem:—

1. **By repressing thoughts and feelings and making choices out of Fear rather than out of growth**. Doing things because you are afraid not to do them, rather than because you want to do them.

   Both motivations will get you there. Why are you doing what you are doing?

2. **By devaluing your resources, minimizing your choices and any decisions that you make**, e.g. what is going to happen will happen, so I believe that I have no choice. These are coming from negative thoughts, beliefs, attitudes, feelings and choices. Doom and gloom is based on the belief that you no longer have any choices.

   With this comes the lowering of your "values". You base your evaluation on things such as punctuality and manners. "I am a wonderful person because...." Evaluation is no longer made on principles. Once you did have high values (quality) but these were lowered. Quantity is now more important than quality.

3. **Seeking esteem through aspiration and intention**, e.g. "when I have some time off I will...." You appraise on intention. You think of yourself as impressive, important, valuable based on intention. Because you aspire you want the credit now—the payoff. "I did not intend to burn the house down, so therefore I do not feel responsible for it". "I intend to treat you this way, therefore you should treat me as though I have" are examples

of this type of thinking. This thinking leaves you wide open to being a Martyr too—through vindication in the future.

4.   The most frequent of all is **seeking outside validation** as a source of Self Esteem. This is devastating not to mention painful, competitive, expensive, time consuming, distracting and dishonest to who you are, e.g.

- you get your approval from having the right body shape,
- the right job,
- the right car,
- possessions with the right labels on them,
- knowing the right people,
- eating in the right restaurants,
- seeing the right movies at the right time,
- attending the right opening nights of the right plays,
- wearing the right combination of colors at the right time,
- having the right hairstyle,
- living at the right address,
- reading the right best sellers,
- traveling to the right destinations for holidays,
- knowing the right people,
- having the right interior designer or dress maker,
- coming from the right background (and not the other side of the tracks),
- sending your children to the right schools (then there's that whole living through the success of your children syndrome or just forcing them to live out your unfulfilled dreams).

We have all seen one-up-manship and have practiced it most when we have been most afraid and vulnerable and lacking in self confidence. It is false confidence because it is based on an illusion.

So you value yourself based on what the outside world sees and thinks of you—or at east what you think it thinks of you. The source of your Self Esteem should be because you approve of you. Outside validation otherwise is OK e.g. work is validated by a paycheck, an actor's performance is critiqued by a critic or his peers—he actually needs that validation. That is validation for a job well done. It is wonderful to have aspirations but use them as a motivation not as a replacement for true Self Esteem. Akin to this is a desire to be perfect. Once perfect you think that you are "right" and therefore deserving of Love. The fashion and advertising industries were built on this type of Fear of people not being right. It is all about status, status symbols and snobbery. Hence the adage—money doesn't bring happiness—and that is one of the reasons why. There's nothing wrong with money in itself at all. If anything it is a symbol of power—a symbol of the ability to act. In many ways being over weight is not about diet but about not being perfect and therefore believing that you are not deserving. It is a form of self punishment. Not in all cases—but most. And overweight can be as little as one pound over your idea of ideal. It can be many other things too. A cry for help, a sense of defeat and the need to feel protection from the outside world.

Stop for a moment and think about what is Self Esteem really and make a personal evaluation and identify which of the four false esteems you most frequently use. Do not use these insights as sources of Self Pity but as motivation to change.

12.325 What happens when you start relying on false esteem?

1. **You become riddled with anxiety, worry, doubt, and confusion.** These are by degree and can lead to totality in their extreme. It becomes the confusion, doubt etc. in your life. That never quite finishes. Anxiety is Fear of the future—and if that dress and those baubles aren't "right" for that gala event or you're afraid that Betty down the road is going to out shine you then you can see why you would be worried.

2. **You insatiably try to fulfill the four sources of Self Esteem.** You reduce your thoughts/feelings with others and your standards etc. What you need to do gets bigger and bigger with more and more intentions. It never ends. "Better this" and "better that" becomes a mantra and a way of life. By degree you move from simple through to obsession/addiction. It takes over who you are. You become your Negative Ego.

You've seen the type—cool, calculating, too nice, too sweet, too much, too acerbic. You know they are holding a metaphorical knife behind their backs.

3.   **You end up feeling powerless**. Your esteem hangs in the balance. It is the opinion of you by others that matters not yours. You depend on them for validation and being. You will lead a life of misery always wanting and waiting for their approval. You no longer cause your life to happen in that positive sense of cause but are driven by Fear and what you think may be noble and good reasons to perform.

4.   Constantly **waiting to wake up from the nightmare** or to the nightmare of your reality. Your life never goes away. Day after day nothing much changes. You're imprisoned and even if you go away on holidays it manages to catch up with you one way or another. You can't run away from life.

5.   Beyond the misery and powerlessness **you get caught in your own depression and Anger**, you become bitter, cynical, resentful, imprisoned in a reality that you feel is beyond your control. There's no Love so you feel these off spring of Fear.

6.   **You become totally physically exhausted**. You are so tired of running. It is draining your energy trying to keep everything in your reality in place. It's all too much. You retreat into the escapism of problems larger than you—soap operas, TV dramas, the bad news on TV and in the press and give up in powerlessness to problems that you have created as part of the mass consciousness and which you can't afford to have go away. Once a problem is solved another appears. It's endless and goes on forever. Now we have new diseases (AIDS) to replace the old ones (polio).

7.   In the midst of your exhaustion **you become totally competitive**. You say to your reality "it is now not enough that you approve of me, it is only me that you can approve of. My aspirations have to be the best, wiser, one more than you." Silent competition is the usual way that it is done. You never admit

the competition. There is no start or finish line so you cannot see it. You have to have more but have to compete to get it. This is distorted male energy and the world of the Ego—basically Earth today. It is the insecure Fear based lives of many people. Everything just keeps getting faster and faster. More, more, more characterized by the questions—"what is the latest? What is the best?" take a moment to observe car commercials—that hallmark of masculinity (the motorized horse)—and you'll see what I mean.

It never ends, leading from disturbing you to ultimately destroying you.

12.326   What happens when you rely on the proper way to positive Self Esteem?

1. **You become alive,** i.e. feeling Love, trust, expectancy and enthusiasm. It is the corner stone of good health. You no longer feel the effects of Fear.

2. **You become really creative,** i.e. generating or stimulating conception and perception. Conceiving something new or getting a deeper sense of understanding. It can be artistic or just a conversation. This creativity will flow onto others. Your energy then attracts similar people to you.

3. **Pleasure, happiness and joy** start to show up in your life.

4. **Your spirituality takes on a dynamic aliveness.** You open yourself to your future and Higher Self.

5. **Feel a sense of pride in what you have done physically, emotionally and intellectually.** A sense of accomplishment. Now you can feel that sense of value. Positive pride as opposed to the arrogance of defensive self-protection. Your Ego now only gets what you give it and pride, which was negative in the hands of Ego, is now a self-respect that comes from true self-confidence.

6. **A sense of productivity.** Whatever you do you learn something about yourself. That is what productivity is—doing something in such a way so that you learn something

more about yourself. Not being pre-occupied with self-protection you can now go out into the world unafraid and develop your potential with grace and the expectancy of success—not the sabotage of Martyr or lack of deserving of Self Pity.

7.   **You will feel a willingness to venture and adventure** to new challenges, chances and opportunities. The Fear is gone.

12.327   How do you seek legitimate Self Esteem? What do you do?

1.   **Release your parents**. Let them be a human. Fragile, frail and real. Do not insist that they match up to some child's idea of superman. The absent parent who was not there, emotionally or literally has wounded some people. That has knocked the wind out of you, so that you have had to rely on the macho/chauvinistic model of father to try and fill the hole left by the absence or the weak/emotional model of mother. They are not coming back to fill the hole. You have to fill it and let go of it. Give them permission to make mistakes, to be fallible, to be a failure, to be frightened. You have earned Love from your father. Mother's Love was given.

2.   **Between the ages of 7 and 10** is the most important time as it was during this time that you established your patterns of Self Esteem. At this time father is discovered. What did you do in that age group? Deal with the child there. What traumas, fantasies, evaluations, secrets, pains and hurts were there? What happened and what did it do to the qualities of esteem in terms of your determination to be powerful/powerless? For some of us it was in that age group that some of us gave up, got hurt, got left out, had bad grades, were sickly, had a fall; what was a major event at that time that affected your Self Esteem? Was it principle/expediency that inspired your motivation? Were you able to integrate, understand? Become the child in meditation and work through it as the now healed balanced self. In that meditation be the friend, therapist, big

brother, counselor and big sister that you did not have to help you through the traumas.

3. **Identify and release the false Self Esteem**. Recognize, acknowledge, forgive and change it. Be compassionate with yourself. You have been angry and isolated and perhaps didn't even know it—you've been doing it so long. Little wonder men have Fear of commitment.

4. **Measure, appraise, evaluate and estimate your value.**
    i) How honest are you? That corresponds with your determination to be powerful. Honesty is the determination to be powerful. Measure your honesty daily, weekly or however.
    ii) Responsibility. How willingly am I taking responsibility? We all are taking responsibility to some extent, even though there are some of us who are postponing it with disastrous results, e.g. taking it in one big gulp as in cancer, AIDS, heart disease. This corresponds to your ability to think and feel.
    iii) Integrity is the spontaneousness with which you take responsibility and if you have to wonder whether you have it or not, then you do not. How spontaneous are you? Evaluate it. This can be done in hindsight. It corresponds to character.
    iv) Trust. How much do you trust yourself? How many around you are worthy of trust? You are not judging them but having an opinion. To be judgmental is to assess their evolution. Evaluate them e.g. if they were worthy of being trusted but you were afraid to—low marks; if they were not worthy of trust but you trusted them anyway—low marks; if they were worthy of trust and you did trust them—high marks. You trusted yourself because there was a basis of trust not just blind trust but honest trust. That corresponds to a willingness and a desire to understand. Never

underestimate willingness. It is one of the most powerful feelings in the Universe. More than you can imagine at the moment.

5.   **Evaluate your co-creation of reality**. How much today did I work with the Universe or the higher aspects of my consciousness? Have you been listening to the whispers of your reality, i.e. looking at the clues and hints that your beliefs have been creating for you to experience and have you been taking account of them? This evaluation corresponds to evaluating your motivation—is it based on principle or expedience?

6.   **How much do you honor your emotions** without letting them run your life? How much do you integrate your emotions/feelings?

7.   **Looking at your life and being able to consciously say that I have not hurt anyone**. Powerless people hurt people. That is how they get their power. They de-base you.

Evaluate yourself regularly by way of these seven points and you will have Self Esteem. It will develop on its own if you do it honestly. Self Esteem gives you what you need to do today. The doom and gloomers will create their own doom, eradicating every source of Self Esteem, forcing themselves and those around them to turn to the false senses. With Self Esteem you will have the right to be here. Release your Guilt around that.

12.4   SATSANG

This is my favorite and the best as it is the most efficient practice of all. If you did this and nothing else you would not have to do anything else to become whole, to heal, to know who you were, to freely choose your life, to have it all. I love satsang for its simplicity. It is the art of doing nothing itself. Anyone can do it but not everyone can do it. The conundrum is that it is easy enough to be done by anyone but many people can't bear to do nothing. It drives them crazy.

Like yoga, satsang is an Indian practice. A master giver of satsang, Isaac Shapiro, describes satsang as "a meeting with Truth. What is spoken of as Truth is That which doesn't change. We have many different experiences, but something remains the same. This is what's called Truth. That which is always here. That which doesn't change."

It is a situation where people gather together with the intention of meeting themselves. For those people who are still Mind focused—such as most of the western world—satsang is very foreign, challenging and easily dismissed. It is still almost unheard of in America.

In my experience the essence of satsang is sitting and doing nothing, so that eventually the Mind quietens completely to a point of stillness. The head is empty. At this point you step outside your Mind into a new paradigm. An even bigger picture than the one I have painted here in this book. In this new paradigm there is nothing. It is the void between the universes. It is where there is no time, no form, nothing. Just Isness.

The practice occurs where a person holds satsang. It is an event. This person is someone who has realized the self. In the stillness of this person's vibration, the participants sit normally or on the floor if they wish. It is very casual. The surroundings are immaterial. As the person at the head of the room becomes quieter within themselves, your vibration also becomes quieter. And that is it. You are welcome to speak one at a time and the participants will ask questions of the person at the front of the room. The information forthcoming is almost always perfect for the people in the room. It is like a large audience with God for your benefit. You really get that life is an illusion.

There's none of the effusiveness and commercial spin offs that are traditionally associated with the New Age, especially in America. People are very calm. They are down to earth. There's none of this dressing up as a new age person like flowing white robes or velvet with silver locketed pendants of Merlin and other new age paraphernalia. It is extremely normal. Typically the attendee has been on the spiritual path for many many years and has now reached this point. The average age is more like 50 than 35. These are people who in the main know themselves, are very comfortable with that, some are still looking for answers while the others just love being in the space and energy that satsang creates. It is blissful. And everything in your life works itself out. You really do not have to do much. Your intuition becomes very advanced and you get a sense of what needs to be done. You forget everything that is of no importance at all. The Mind completely clears of its chatter and needless need to remember everything. It is most de-stressing. With the Mind rested it awakens sharper and fresher and clearer to be your servant again. Usually admission is by donation.

There are some noted international givers of Satsang. Isaac Shapiro (www.geocities.com/Athens/Thebes/2689/home), Ranjit Maharaj, an 87 year old strict Advaitan with about 70 years of deepening presence around him (a great master) is at www.sadguru.com or try www.hindunet.org/srh_home/1997_5/0101.html or Ken Johnson, Eckhart Tolle (namaste@bc.sympatico.ca), Vartman (www.vartman.com) and Gungaji (www.gangaji.org/satsang/welcome). The satsang that I speak of is based on the teaching of Ramana Maharshi and Papaji who belong to the Advaitan School of philosophy. In previous centuries Jesus, Buddha, Ibn El'Arabi, Br. Lawrence, Hakuin, H Hsin Ming, O. Khayyan, Mirabai, Rinzai, Jalaluddin Rumi and Zhuangzi belonged to this philosophy of study called Advaitan. Some of the names will be familiar but to the non-philosopher most will not.

Search the web for "satsang" for contacts in your area particularly for givers of satsang who teach from Ramana. These will be sites pertaining to Amber, Advashanti, Arjuna, R Balsekar, Douglas Harding, Catherine Ingram, Eli Jaxon-Bear, F Lucile, Sailor Bob, Scott Morrison, Toni Packer, Shanti Mayi, Galen Sharp, Esther Veltheim and Ram Tze as well as the people I have already mentioned.

These people travel for most of the year such is the demand for their presence. Most visits occur in Australia and Europe with very few and limited stops in North America. These people specialize in delivering enlightenment and many time I have seen people "get it" on their first visit. It is a wonderful experience. You will learn that "happiness is a still Mind".

In time and with practice you do not need to attend satsang. You can reach that place of stillness yourself.

If you can't do satsang do Byron Catie's "The Work". For the best results do both together. One substitute's for the other when satsang isn't available in your town. In many ways then almost everything else in this Division becomes redundant because satsang is the pot of gold. It does away with having to process out your belief system and getting in touch with your emotional blockages. These burn out of your Subconscious with the light of the Universe that is delivered through satsang. While the effects of yoga are also physical and it is a physical practice in opening the chakras, satsang is done in stillness and there is no movement. You just sit or lie down.

The latest book on what can be found in living in the now is by Eckhart Tolle in his wonderful contribution called *The Power of Now: A Guide to Spiritual Enlightenment* printed in 1999 by New World Library. He wrote his book following a experience of divine intervention. For those of you who are seeking more—this book is the next step on your progress. It picks up where I leave off. It's fabulous for really taking you into a new way of living. An oh so much better way than being in Fear.

Chapter 13

—Using Vibrational Medicine

13.1 INTRODUCTION

What we are beginning to see is that each organ and system in the body is calibrated to absorb and process specific energies. So when we are all whole we are said to be "in tune". Where the frequency is not normal there is the potential for disease. Vibrational medicine is the name given to the modalities that work on re-tuning the body by using energy to do so—not the mechanics of Newtonian medicine. In other words you can't see what is being done because the doing is on energy fields that can't be seen by the naked eye. In the old days it might have been called "faith healing". Or in the 19th Century dismissed as some Eastern gibberish for it includes Chinese & Ayuervedic Medicine and acupuncture, all of which are thousands of years old, Reiki and homeopathy as well as the mystical treatments of channeling and crystals. They fix the frequencies, which hold the body in place.

There was developed in the 1990's a machine into which was input the frequency of healthy organs from a physical body. In the case of a person who was not well electrodes were placed on the acupuncture points relating to the specific organ. An electrical frequency was then run into the body using the body's own electrical pathways to raise the frequency of the organ which was diseased.

This effected a healing of the organ. The machine was featured on *Chicago Hope* in 1994 and was used on comedian Richard Pryor whose MS was so bad that he could not raise his head of his pillow. After treatments he was able to perform on stage at the Comedy Store on Sunset Boulevard in Los Angeles.

This is type of 21st Century medicine that I was referring to at the conclusion to Chapter 4.

So far as I am concerned the leading book on this subject is *Vibrational Medicine: New Choices for Healing Ourselves* by Richard Gerber published in 1988 by Bear & Co. There has since been printed a revised edition which will tell you about 714X, a Canadian antioxidant treatment which cures cancer. Gerber, a physician and scientist, combines the best scientifically proven theory and marries it with all the vagueness of the ancient healing arts which have never been understood but which have worked for centuries. He proves why they do. It is a very detailed but inspiring and conclusive study in its depth. Definitively and intelligently it examines the scientific basis for homeopathy, flower essence treatments, crystal healing, the chakras, acupuncture, radionics, electro therapy, herbal medicine, laying on of hands and therapeutic radiology.

The following sub-chapters are various well known modalities. There are more than enough books available on these subjects for you to study them to your heart's content. I will mention them just briefly to give you an idea as to what they are about.

If you don't believe me as to how invasive alternative remedies now are go to AOL Health and you'll see a vast amount of information and feedback from patients on what is and the effects of Acupuncture, Aromatherapy, Ayuervedic Medicine, Homeopathy, the Energy System connection, Oriental Medicine, Reiki and Yoga. Or just look in your average newspaper or health magazine and you will always find a reference to alternative medicines.

13.2 Visualization

Louis Proto in his book *Self Healing* published by Judy Piatkus (Publishers) Limited adequately describes visualization and affirmations. As does Shakti Gwain in her classic book *Creative Visualization*. Louise Hay also makes great use of it as well. In fact it is probably the most commonly used new age technique. Knowing that imagination is the key to reality creation you can understand why it is.

Visualizing is just that. Imagining what you want or how you want it to be. It is envisioning. If you have cancer then imagine the tumor becoming smaller. If you are body building imagine the muscles getting bigger as you lift. If you are a golfer imagine the ball going exactly where you want it to be. If you have a viral infection imagine a vacuum cleaner in your body vacuuming up the virus. This stuff really does work. Anything that you can think of can be imagined. By thinking it you have already imagined it. It is the power of positive thinking. It is stage one of reality creation.

13.3 Homeopathy

This is one of the greatest modalities for healing the Energy Bodies. It is truly a marvelous science. The effects are profound—overnight in some cases—deep and long lasting. Ideally it is used as a preventive medicine having the ability to seek out and identify potential illness in you then treating it before it manifests physically.

The treatment is administered by a homeopath. It is a natural system of medicine using almost any inorganic or organic basis in minute quantities to create changes in the energy field of the body. The more diluted the concentration of remedy the more powerful it is. The potion triggers the body's natural ability to heal itself. Application is by taking drops under the tongue in anything from one to a few dosages over one or a few days. It is that simple.

A remedy is chosen for its ability to rebalance the body by giving it the frequency that it needs. The body assimilates the energy boost, throws off the toxicity and the patient recovers.

13.4 Non-Human Energy—The Devas, Astrology & Numerology

Ever wondered why you feel better after a day in the outdoors—especially in a forest, a park or at the beach?

The devas are those energies which exist in the world and which are responsible for each species of plant, mineral, animal and machine taking physical form and functioning. Just as the chakras step down or transformer like reduce the higher frequencies of our energy bodies into our physical body such is the same function of the devas. Therefore they are the equivalent of the chakras in the non-human world. You see just as we have energy fields so do all other objects on Earth.

Dolphins are devic in nature. They are transformers. Ever wonder why they are always smiling and playing and why people are so drawn to them almost as mythical creatures and why there are so many stories of them having rescued humans at sea? They are full of the higher vibrating energy.

To take advantage of the Devic energy you need to go to where it is strongest, most rampant, free and untamed. It is the life force. Sitting in the ocean or a rain forest or a mountain will work. Bushland, rolling hills, a farm is excellent, a park or even working in a garden. Gardeners and farmers tend to have long lives. This is why. It is very much about being in the now. It is very meditative work. Conversely then big cities are not very healthy as the level of devic energy is low. This explains people's love of flowers and plants and parks. In so many ways we are those things that we see. The energy is just the same.

So as to complete an explanation of energy as we know it let me say that the Solar System is an energy field with its various energy bodies being the 12 planets and the sun. Each of these resonates to emit a different frequency. These frequencies in turn affect us. That is the true basis of astrology. Some of us are more impacted by this planet or that planet in us. The star patterns also have their own frequencies and the impact of these are considered in relation to each of the planets. In many ways, there is some truth to the saying "it is written in the stars". I believe that astrology is a guide to giving us a blue print of the Unconscious patterns that we have taken on at the time of our birth, after that it is up to us as to how we work in that energy. All the while though, that initial blueprint is impressed by the movements about earth of the planets. In so many ways outer space is such a direct reflection of the Unconscious.

Just as astrology is a blue print at birth to guide you—a starting point for knowing who you are—so too is numerology and palmistry. A fantastic book on numerology—one that takes the subject to the next level—and has its basis in case studies, is Dan Millman's Book *The Life You Were Born To Live: A Guide To Finding Your Life Purpose* published in 1993 by H J Kramer Inc. Millman is famous for his earlier book *The Way of the Peaceful Warrior*. His numerology book traces your development through the life stages. In numerology each number from 1 to 9 and 11 and 22 are given significance. To obtain your number, add up the numbers from your date of birth, e.g. you are born 23 July 1966. This is 2+3+7 (being the 7th month)+1+9+6+6=34. Then add these numbers together to get the number 7. A '7' person is here to learn about Trust and Openness. But as the 7 is a combination of the 3 and 4 the issues that have first to be learned are expression & sensitivity first then stability and progress. Or as he puts it "to work through issues of trust, patience, and emotional expression and to have faith in the spiritual process operating within their life, establishing security by finding practical ways to contribute to others." The book is very insightful and worth the read.

13.5   Crystals & Atlantis

Any new age store worth its salt will have a range of crystals on display and for sale. These are an icon of the New Age. Yet do you know why?

The belief here is that crystals hold, focus, amplify, conduct and emanate energy—emotional and mental. As everything is energy then certain crystals have the ability to resonate to correct emotional and mental disorders. They are like the electro machine I described in the second paragraph of this Chapter. Primarily they amplify thought energy.

In Atlantis, the lost high technology civilization, energy was stored in crystals. In particular a giant crystal known as the Unfed Light (or Maxin) which powered the continent. To touch it was deadly. Today our computer scientists are beginning to use crystals (silicon) to store information and to use that information in machines—computers. This is another example of science catching up with fantasy.

Atlantis is such a fascinating story that it deserves to be told very briefly here if for no other reason than as an analogy or warning. It is said to have existed from 150,000 BC to 9,600 BC. Plato's story comes from Solon, the law maker of Athens in 600BC. He had obtained the information from the Egyptian priests. The Great Pyramid and the Sphinx were ancient 2,000 years ago when the Romans were there and this was after the Greeks. In fact Egypt was an Atlantean colony, as well as Eastern Europe (before there was a Western Europe), North, South and Central America as well as in Tibet and other parts of Africa. It is said that a record of the Atlantean civilization is stored below the Great Sphinx and that when mankind is ready (=mature enough) that this information will be discovered.

The subcontinent of Atlantis is below the Atlantic Ocean. Over a long period a series of earthquakes broke the land up until finally the continent vanished under the sea. These same earthquakes sank $2/3^{rd}$ of what is now Australia, the remainder of that continent now being under the Pacific Ocean. At the time Australia was known as Lemuria and this was the great civilization that preceded Atlantis and which was eventually destroyed by it. This was not before the Atlanteans had developed impressive technology—driverless cars, flying machines that could circle the earth in a day and act as submarines too, reading machines that spoke to you, television and x-ray but to name a few. It is said that there once were 13 planets but a laser gun developed by the Atlanteans destroyed one of them. This planet was left as rubble and is now known as the Asteroid Belt. Such was the damage that the sun was blacked out and this in fact caused the dinosaurs to die.

The seeds of vibrational medicine are in Atlantis. One of their greatest discoveries was the power that exists in sunlight and the subtle energetic effect that this has had on life itself. They tapped into this and used this to power their civilization. They discovered the healing power of colored light and built temples of healing that used light. The Egyptians did too. This may explain why so many ancient civilizations worshipped the sun—through a convolution of passing down the information from the more advanced (but long since extinct) civilizations, the later ones only knew that light was the key to all life.

The Atlanteans knew how to grow crystals and used them to amplify the sun's rays into useable power. Isn't that what a magnifying glass does? Laser surgery is no different.

The problem with Atlantis was that its energy became imbalanced. The prevailing energy became one of Mind and spiritual energy waned. The Minds of the Atlanteans became so strong that they lost touch with their feelings and became very war like. Slavery of a less intellectual peoples developed. It was a civilization that lost its way morally and eventually imploded just as the land below its feet exploded destroying it.

America is said to be strongly populated by peoples who have reincarnated from the late Atlantean age. They are said to be here at this time in our discovery of technology to ensure that the mistakes of Atlantis are not repeated and that we retain our spiritual balance.

13.6 Channeling

This is a growth area. And one that I have had extensive experience with. Channeling is the technique whereby a person is able to tune into a higher frequency or vibration of energy of the Energy System and using the skills of one or more of clairaudience, clairvoyance or clairsentience they act as a receiver (much like a radio and aerial) and see, feel or hear the messages and images and sounds coming from those higher frequencies. These higher frequencies include the Sub-conscious, Unconscious, your Spirit Guides, your Higher Self, other aspects of you (like the child, the adolescent, the Shadow and the other entities you have created inside you), past lives and the higher aspects of your consciousness.

With this ability, a channel can tell you not only what you are think-ing but what you are not conscious of and may not be able to be con-scious of, e.g. because you are numb to your feelings or the information exists in an energy field outside your Emotional Body (i.e. at a higher frequency) or because your Ego is dominating your consciousness.

The practitioners of this art are few and far between—but more are becoming known. The one best known to me is Patricia Brennan author of *Facing The Dawn: Awakening Your True Potential* (1995) by Harper Collins and *Vision & Heart: Creating Balance & Harmony In Your Life* (1996) by Harper Collins and *Stress First Aid Kit* (1999) by Inside Out Publishing (www.lifethemes.com). We worked together during much of the 1990's.

A good channeler can save you months, even years in therapy. Usually within a hour you can find out the beliefs behind why things are happening in your life, why you are as you are, what issues you need to be dealing with, your denials, where your behavior is coming from, medical conditions, your dreams and even your optimum future. Dreams are messages from your Sub-conscious, which uses symbols to communicate with you.

Usually the session will make no sense to the channel but are per-fectly understood by the person having the session.

13.7   Tao

This is a rejuvenating Chinese discipline based on martial arts principles and which uses the energy of the chakras to fortify the body. There are many techniques. The simplest is the Inner Smile—you sit on the edge of a chair and visualize a ball of energy the size of a baseball starting at the base of your spine. Visualize it moving up your spine, moving around the top of your head down your face and the front of your body in an elongated circle to the point of commencement. It works. After a weekend workshop I was energized for days. It works best with practice and provides long term results. It is also a very good philosophy. I know one person whose hair started to grow back after doing it and who looks late 30's but is in fact late 40's!!

13.8   Acupuncture

This is from Japan and China. Personally I prefer the Japanese method—it doesn't hurt as much. The body is cris-crossed with meridians that conduct energy. These are linked directly to the hundreds of mini chakras in the body. At the same time they are linked by electrical circuitry to the internal organs. These are the acupuncture points that are found on the skin. Each part of the body corresponds to an internal organ.

The procedure involves sticking a very fine needle just under the skin. This conducts the electrical current in the meridian from the energy body into the physical body. Once the needle is in there is no discomfort. Acupuncture has become so accepted that even Western doctors are administering it in their surgeries in conjunction with western treatments.

13.9 Aromatherapy

This is the beautiful side of healing. As the name implies it is therapy based on smell or aroma. For thousands of years herbs have been a source of prescription for healing. The properties of various herbs have been shown to work on various diseases, heal cuts and sores. These herbs have been combined with oil and are massaged into the body. So there are two benefits. Massage to physically move the blocked energy out of the physical body and herbs that enter the body through the skin—the largest organ in the body. If you have never had aromatherapy do yourself a favor and go out and make a booking now. It is nurturing and does wonders for your sense of well being. A good masseur can use his fingers to find blockages of energy within the body and release them.

13.10 Ayuervedic Medicine

This is the ancient practice of the Hindus. Being up to 5,000 years old it assess people on their body types and treats them according to their characteristics. The theory being that certain energies manifest in particular forms and if all of one type of people get particular illnesses then this must be attributed to their energy. All of us have an aspect of the three body types. Ayuervedic medicine is used as a lifestyle and as a diagnostic tool. Deepak Chopra in his book *Perfect Weight* (1991) published by Random House, explains Ayurveda in the context of weight control claiming that there is no such thing as weight for height but rather weight for type should be used as the criteria.

BODY TYPE	PHYSICAL CHARACTERISTICS	SYMPTOMS OF IMBALANCE
VATA – related to the energy of air and body movements – vocal chords, thought, blood hands and feet	• light, thin build • works fast & energy comes in bursts • not a heavy sleeper & sleeps at odd times • bright, enthusiastic, full of energy • learns fast but tends to worry • gets tired quickly and burns out • doesn't eat regularly & gets hungry at odd times	• insomnia • worry • under weight • tension headaches • constipation • arthritis • dry or rough skin
PITTA – related to the energy of fire and controls the metabolism and digestion regulating hunger, thirst, heat and intelligence	• medium build, endurance and strength • fair complexion and dislikes hot weather & the sun • can't skip meals & is hungry before them • talks precisely & is smart • enterprising person who hates having his time wasted • angry or irritable under stress • hot & thirsty when waking in the night • learns from experience, is sarcastic or critical at times • is commanding and walks determinedly	• rashes & skin diseases • visual problems • premature graying or balding • heartburn
KAPHA – related to the energy of water and earth and controls the body's structure, bones, cells, muscles and tendons	• solid powerful build with great strength • steady energy & a slow graceful action • relaxed and slow to Anger • good retentive memory but slow to learn • heavy sleeper and probe to obesity • affectionate, tolerant, forgiving, complacent • feels empathy and is conciliatory • cool, smooth, thick, pale and often oily skin	• obesity • slow digestion • allergies • depression • laziness • asthma • joint problems

For a thoroughly detailed explanation of Ayuervedic medicine and its life style philosophy you should read the outstanding work of Dr. Vinod Verma's *Ayurveda. A Way of Life* (1995) published by Samuel Webster Inc. There is a compete explanation given on health in relation to color, form, sensation, smell, cleansing the body inside and out, revitalization through massage and yoga, the effects of habits in eating, alcohol and tobacco, the differences between and the effects of suppressible and non-suppressible urges, remedies and the prevention of ailments, the properties of herbs and their healing qualities, remedies and the prevention of illness.

Conclusion

That completes this book. Congratulations on having reached this point. While the book is very small it is very intense and covers a lot of material.

I hope that it is clear to you now how the Negative Ego feeds on Fear and Anger to keep you separate from that which you deny yourself to be and in doing so keeping you from being whole and being able to access Love. In doing this the Ego causes you pain and suffering. The path to enlightenment is to follow the path of Love, relinquish Fear as the motivator of your reality and to take responsibility for all parts of your life.

In my next book I take the Metaphysical Model which **HOW TO HAVE A BETTER LIFE** develops, and apply it to HIV and AIDS—diseases which are very closely related to cancer in their cause—deep Anger.

In this new book you will see how Fear and Anger in conjunction with the Shadow and the Ego worked together to produce AIDS. HIV is a warning that AIDS will come if you don't change your beliefs. HIV does not necessarily cause AIDS.

From the combination of the Fear and Anger of Ego came powerlessness, helplessness, hopelessness, defensiveness and defenselessness. These conditions led to AIDS. The Anger was bound into low Self Esteem, Guilt, Self Pity and Victimhood. Underscoring these energies were the beliefs of the Victims themselves. There is no blame or judgment here. Conspiracy theories were the physical outplays of the beliefs of the gay culture and it's fixation of being

Victims—which in itself was part of the cause of the disease. The book explores what was really going on in the gay world because it was here that the disease had its roots—in the psyche of the sub-culture—in their collective belief structure.

The book will be very confronting to anyone who does not believe that they create their own reality—these are people who do not take responsibility for their lives and who are still blaming other people for the disease and are still giving their power away seeking cures from limited sources instead of owning up to the fact that they were creating the disease all along.

About the Author

Stephen was a corporate lawyer before being a production manager, television commercial producer, director, producer and marketing manager in the advertising and film industry. Later he set up private legal practices devoted to helping low income earners. Today he hosts a self help talk back radio show in Los Angeles.